CW01023481

Published by: Landon Publishing

First Edition

Copyright Graeme Milne 2022

ISBN 978-1-915787-13-2

Dedication

To my fabulous wife Carol and my lovely daughters Tabitha and Geri. To my grandson Liam, my brothers Alan and Robert and to Mum and Dad, bless you as always. Also respectively dedicated to Dod Copland, an original Aberdeen punk and a true spiritualist who will be much missed.

Acknowledgements

A massive thank you to all who contributed their stories to this book without your input it would never have happened. Also, a big thank you to staff at Edinburgh Central Library who went above and beyond the call of duty. Thanks also to The Edinburgh Evening News and Liam Rudden for their support. A big shout out also to John S. Tantalon of North Edinburgh Nightmares, Jamie Corstorphine at City of the Dead Tours, David B, Esje at the Banshee Labyrinth (possibly the most haunted pub in Scotland) Mark Edward Wilson, the University of Edinburgh and the Society for Psychical Research. Also, good wishes to Mark Fernyhough and Susan Sloan, two Edinburgh friends who appreciate a good ghost story and to John Thrower for many good conversations on the Royal Mile. Last but certainly not least, thanks to my fellow guides, Alasdair, Alvaro, Cinitia, Emma, Fernando, Fraser, Glen, Graeme, Katie, Kat, Kenny, Paul, Rory, Ryan and Sara who all tell a good story but are rarely recompensed, without them the city would be a poorer place. There are many others, who as of now will have to remain anonymous, but you know who you are, and I thank for your contributions.

Cauld blaws the nippin 'north wi' angry sough
An' showers his hailstanes frae the cast cleugh
 Owre the Grayfriars, where at mirkest hour
 Bogles and Spectres wont to tak their tour

Robert Ferguson: Ghaists, a Kirk-Yard Eclogue

I best you sometime wonder
What is standing right behind you
Keep looking over your shoulder to see if it's there
For some the church bell pealing
For some the risk of feeling and stealing
Quietly alone, through the night looking under your bed

Francis Monkman (Curved Air) Phantasmagoria

Table of Contents

Introduction

Edinburgh has long been regarded as one of Europe's most haunted cities and on the face of it, with its dimly lit alleys and ancient streets it looks the part, but is it really? And more importantly are the oft repeated stories true? I would suggest yes or at least in part. The ghost tour industry certainly plays its part and as far as promoting its' ghosts, the city has a very loud voice indeed. No other city quite sells its ghosts like Edinburgh. Paranormal investigation, once the hobby of pipe-smoking eccentrics has now become omnipresent. The internet is increasingly clogged with supposed 'investigations' and in doing so has designated the study of 'real' ghosts to sideshow status. This of course does not contribute in any way to the big question, that being what lies beyond the veil? The once solitary pursuit of investigating 'haunted houses' is no more. Today on television the discerning viewer is subjected to an unappealing mixture of jump scares and self-aggrandising which has heaped further indignity onto the subject. For example, take our ghost hunting chums of yesteryear. Most, with a few notable exceptions, shunned publicity preferring to carry out their research in isolation taking a vaguely academic approach to the subject. The 'tech' back then, rudimentary by today's standards would invariably consist of a half-chewed pencil, notebook and flask and perhaps a homely Briar. And why not? Smoking was heartily encouraged. The company of a four-legged companion might also be employed serving the purpose of an early alarm system. Times certainly have changed, and despite being left cold by the circus that constitutes a modern investigation, I concede that for a modern audience the sight of a well-dressed chap observing quietly would perhaps make poor viewing.

Auld Reekie, capital of Scotland is a city at least by appearance, that deserves to be haunted. It is a wonderfully atmospheric playground for those interested in the esoteric and its' reputation precedes itself. Today, while traversing it's many 'closes,' it's easy to start believing in those old wives' tales from the past, even though the authentic spookiness of old continues to shrink under the light of scrutiny. I can however promise, that within those foreboding alleyways there are still shadows that no amount of light can pierce. Sadly, the original habitants are long gone now replaced by a transient population, but despite this it is heartening to know that perhaps not all the original residents have moved on. In the following pages I hope to demonstrate this. Many of the stories, I am happy to report are current and therefore have been related to me by people still very much alive and able to articulate their own experiences. I have also covered some of Edinburgh's 'old faithful's,' merely to readdress some of the misinformation, and in doing so I trust my retellings have not muddied the waters further. So, at the end of it all the question remains, 'why do people go on a ghost tour?' This is a question that has haunted me, ahem, for many years. We have all been tourists at some point and of course undertaken tours of varying kinds but there is something a little more specialised about a ghost tour. Having an interest however is not a requisite despite what one would imagine, which the following illustrates.

On an average tour, the demographic will consist of around 70% non-believers, 20%, open-minded individuals and 10% believers gained through personal experience or religious grounds. This has the makings of a good tour, but if the group is entirely made up of sceptics, the temptation to weep is strong. Don't get me wrong my task as a guide is not to persuade, though it is helpful to have a few people on board with the concept. After all, if you were teetotal would you join a wine tasting tour? The most dreaded participant however and the one which all guides fear, is the eye roller. Usually situated front and centre they will habitually sigh deeply throughout the tour and display the white of their eyes at every opportunity.

But that is not all, for further adding to the guides misery is the geographic makeup of their group. For example, Americans are usually generous as are Germans, though the latter generally do not hold particularly strong beliefs. However, despite their shyness towards the paranormal they are good tippers and are always welcome on my tour. Some countries however let their side down on two fronts, by being both ghost dodgers and misers. They know who they are, and I will say no more for fear of causing an international incident. There is enough trouble in the world today.

It has been a fascinating journey and I have recorded many hitherto unpublished experiences for posterity, which I hope readers will enjoy reading. Ultimately Edinburgh is in the enviable position of being saturated with tourists and the industry happily meets the demand. To most, the subject is merely a bit of fun and so at the end of the day that is why perhaps most visitors feel obliged to undertake a tour. On that note, please join me now on my ghost tour, where we will attempt to separate fact from fiction as we explore one of the world's most haunted cities!

The Castle

Any tour of Edinburgh would be incomplete without a visit to Britain's most taken castle and so, quite rightly this is our starting point. It has always dominated the city skyline and like any self-respecting castle is obliged to have ghosts. Most are the dyed in the wool types, phantom drummers, ghostly pipers and the like so the seasoned investigator must approach with caution. It does however offer some solid reports along with those of the riper variety. Regarding the latter perhaps the phantom piper is the best known and although undoubtedly an old wife's tale, here goes anyway. The story describes the unfortunate disappearance of a young piper who on being sent to investigate a newly discovered tunnel beneath the castle, vanishes. The date this took place has never been disclosed, but the point of entry to the tunnel was described as too small to admit an adult. Once inside he was then instructed to head down the Royal Mile and to play his pipes, to ascertain the length of the tunnel. Above ground, members of the regiment then followed diligently until the sound of his playing petered out near St. Giles. The story of course ends on a sour note, if you pardon the pun, as nothing was ever heard of the boy again. Today his fate remains a mystery as does the origin of the tale. However, like many dyed in the wool Edinburgh stories there is an unnerving coda, as on certain nights people claim to have heard ghostly piping echoing from below. Duhn! Duhn! Duhn! It is undoubtedly a fanciful legend, though the castle was found to have several tunnels beneath it. The question of course remains, if the lad was playing the pipes, how did he light his way, and would the sound of anyone's playing be audible above? Perhaps I'm being pedantic but subsequent excavations have found no physical evidence to support the story. Despite this however, I was told that a lady on a recent tour apparently fainted at the dénouement of the story, explaining to the guide on her recovery, that she distinctly heard bagpipes. Perhaps it was auto suggestion? Perhaps a real live, flesh and blood busker was playing nearby? Perhaps even this story, will now be repeated for generations to come?

There are however many more plausible stories, and it is to those we now turn to. Take the case of Pamela Hunter once on duty as a bar steward at the castle. On contacting Pamela, she explained to me that one of the most common phenomena reported within the castle walls was the sound of footsteps. Being from no obvious source, the sound has been described as 'disorientating,' for those who have heard them. During the conversation she went onto state that her father also had an experience, while working there. These are her words.

'My dad was also tripped up when walking down past the portcullis gate at the French prison, which is just before the main gate. It was around 2am after the bar was shut, and dad was walking down through the castle. He was pushed from behind and fell forward onto a thin wire which cut across his legs. It was terrifying as there was no one there.'

Not long after another contributor, Linsey Blue, described a similar experience which again I have repeated verbatim. 'I was working during the tattoo one year and I was alone in the officer's mess while the show was on. There were no other staff members on duty apart from me. As I stood there, I noticed a shadow go past the doorway by the bar. I did go and look but there was no one there. I asked the chef about it later when he came in and he claimed it was always like that, but you get used to it. I didn't feel scared, so it didn't bother me that much.' She finished by stating that a common occurrence witnessed by many people were the sounds of ghostly footsteps which were often heard to echo across the courtyard, once visitors have left.

In a similar vein to the young piper, a sentry in 1960 was said to have witnessed a headless drummer on the battlements. Approaching the figure, it slowly turned towards him before vanishing leaving the soldier in a state of shock. In more recent times it has also been claimed that staff in the castle's restaurant may have also inadvertently met the drummer. According to several accounts, the phenomena is most prevalent around an old tunic which is displayed in the café. This has led staff to speculate whether the spirit wore it while he was alive? The garment, a uniform of a Royal Engineer has been described as moving on its own, with its' arm moving up and down as if in the act of drumming. The fact it is housed in a hermetically sealed case, only adds to the mystery.

The castle is also the setting for numerous historic hauntings including the following well-documented case. Having previously read about the story I was keen to know more, and so in due course contacted the Society for Psychical Research (SPR). Formed in 1882, their objective was to scrutinize supposedly spiritual phenomena in a rational scientific manner, keen to cast a critical eye over the superstitions of the past. In a moment of rare synchronicity, the 'new religion' of spiritualism was on the rise and in its wake interest in the paranormal grew exponentially. A conference was held in London in 1882, and it was proposed that an organisation with the express purpose of studying spiritualist phenomena should be created. Publishing quarterly journals detailing their proceedings and case studies, it offered the reader an insight into an unknown world. New scientific breakthroughs in both psychology and physics, shared pages with reports on mediumship and hauntings. It was heady stuff and due to their finding's names like Borley Rectory, commonly referred to as the most haunted house in England, now crept into the public consciousness. For interests' sake, a former president included, W H Salter, whose book 'Ghosts and Apparitions,' is well worth reading. Amusingly he was described as having, 'an odd resemblance to an extremely intelligent and respectable white Aberdeen Terrier,' which being my home city, is a great compliment. The society is still going strong today, though I suspect with developments in science and psychology there is less chance for our current ghosts to manoeuvre. So, with all this in mind and keen to know more I contacted the society who turned out to be very helpful, providing me with details of several letters pertinent to the case.

The author of those letters, a Mrs. Strick, had detailed her experiences and in doing so sent them to a close friend. Somewhere, along the line they then fell into the hands of the SPR. Also worth noting is that the main protagonists, both then resident at the castle have been commonly referred to as Colonel and Mrs. Street but were in fact Colonel and Mrs. Strick, the confusion around their names apparently due to a historic error.

The following account taken from those letters describe their residency at the castle. Subjected to a prolonged haunting from spirits, both human and animal, they make for interesting reading though disappointingly do not include a piper. Despite this she did describe what she saw as 'a shadow the height of a human being,' before claiming, 'the shadow bent down to observe a dustpan and brush left by a maid.' I particularly liked this little detail as I have often speculated what spirits make of modern accoutrements. As an aside, I was reminded of a case I investigated some years ago in an Aberdeen shoe shop, where one of the assistants got quite a scare, when without warning her hoover suddenly lost power. She told me later, that a quick glance revealed that it had been unplugged and as she turned back a small girl's voice could be plainly heard saying, 'What is it? What is it? Referring of course to the hoover. But back to Mrs. Strick.

Further into the letter, she then went onto describe a series of incidents involving what she took to be ghostly cats. I quote: 'I did not see the cats so clearly as the people did in the castle and the cats were never full face, always passing or back view, usually slinking downstairs. They were not transparent I saw them by day and by gaslight. They kept close to the corners of the bannisters just as real cats do, they took no notice of me at all, no one else saw them except one time my husband saw them.'

She also frequently referred to another entity as the 'shadow ghost,' which would intermittently appear and then after a hiatus re-appear, usually on the same spot on the stairs. Her nerves no doubt taxed by these manifestations resulted in her contacting an occultist, as he was described. He then provided a cleansing ceremony, not involving the dustpan we assume, after which the shadow ghosts were vanquished.

Reading on, Mrs. Strick also alluded to the great many semi-feral cats, then living at the castle which she observes were 'making it difficult to differentiate between the living and the dead.' This may have accounted for some of the sightings. The correspondence then stops and as there were no further replies, I was left wondering what happened afterwards or whether the next residents had a quieter tenure. Today we are left to ponder, what secrets still lie within the fabric of this most ancient of structures. With sightings of prisoners, soldiers, animals and even Mary Queen of Scots herself making the odd appearance, it is undoubtedly the perfect setting for any self-respecting ghost. A short walk from the esplanade and we arrive at our next destination.

The Witchery at the Castle

We will now look at the aptly named, 'The Witchery at the Castle,' one of Edinburgh's most sought-after hotels. Incorporating nearby Semple and Jollies close, the twisting staircases, wood panelling and stonework of these ancient buildings create a unique experience for guests. I have been lucky to stay there on more than one occasion and will share my own personal story soon. But first let's travel back in time a little.

The Witchery today, differs than when opened in 1979. Initially building its reputation on the spookiness of the area, it once hosted ghost tours and events and so I was fascinated to discover some newspaper clippings from the early 1980's which described some of the phenomena associated with the building. In the article, related by Charles Cameron and owner James Thomson they described an event which proved to be a little too close to the bone. Cameron, by the way was a well-respected magician and practitioner of bizarre magic and curator of the Edinburgh Wax Museum. This much-missed attraction on the Royal Mile exemplified Edinburgh's love affair with dark history exhibiting lifelike effigies of Burke and Hare, the Wizard of West bow and Deacon Brodie among others. Also, home to a theatre of the bizarre, it became known locally as Dracula's Castle. Cameron, a respected authority on the paranormal was believed to have amassed the largest private collection of books on the subject within the British Isles.

Anyhow in the interview both he and Thomson talked of past events they had hosted and of the property's history. During their conversation they referred to several authentic witchcraft symbols that had been found within the premises. The symbols which were carved into the beams were then described as an ancient language, though how they got there was never touched upon. James went on to say that while working there many real, modern-day witches had visited no doubt keen to see them for themselves. It was because of this; he was in no doubt as to their authenticity. Reading further, they then described holding a Halloween party there, in the early 1980s. On that occasion the owner had invited along an 'expert ghosthunter' as one of the attractions. He went on to explain that during the evening the ghosthunter was asked to recite some incantations in attempt to summon spirits. In hindsight probably not the wisest decision as James explained. 'Suddenly the whole atmosphere changed. The party fun had gone, we felt something strange was happening. It was quite frightening. We won't do it again.' When the reporter pressed for more details, he did not elaborate. There are of course other tales, some already known and others unknown, so here is mine.

I have been fortunate to stay on several occasions, but my first visit was on our wedding and the preceding night. The second night, something of a surprise, was a wedding gift from our friends. It would of course be inconceivable that a building its age, wouldn't have a few ghosts rattling about, but at the time I gave it no thought. I must also add that I felt nothing untoward at first. This however changed as we settled in for our second night in the Armoury Suite.

At first, obviously delighted to be indulging in another night of luxury, our joy was quickly tempered by an unfathomable feeling of oppression which grew stronger as the day wore into night. The rooms were reasonably lit, yet despite this we found it a little daunting to head to the bathroom or further onto the kitchen. At around two in the morning, and unable to sleep I went to make some tea. Carol was asleep and so I crept from the bedroom and headed towards the kitchen. Returning with a cup of tea I found I could not open the door and concerned I would spill the contents; I gingerly began pressing down onto the handle. That was when I first became aware of movement. A sudden noise in a quiet room is disconcerting particularly when it comes from no source. Sudden creaks, soft thuds and the electric buzz of silence are more than likely the result of cooling pipes or settling floorboards, but this was different. The lights were on, and I was fully awake and yet I could hear a soft scraping on the boards directly behind me, and it was getting louder. I glanced backwards my brain unable to compute what was occurring until the source of the noise manifested itself in the form of a dog. It was big, its shaggy grey hair suggesting either a Wolf or Deer Hound and it had appeared out of nowhere. I stood slack-jawed, until with a couple of bounds it stood before me, then vanished. The sound that came from my throat at that moment, I would like to have said was very manly, akin to a caveman grunting but that would have been a lie. It was perhaps more of a whimper but either way the tea was now slopped on the floor, and I was back in the bedroom. My wife still sleeping soundly was undisturbed and I did the decent thing by putting the covers over my head. In the morning I asked how she had slept, and she said, 'terribly,' going on to explain that on waking in the wee small hours she had witnessed a figure standing at the foot of the bed. A quick grope to the left confirmed it wasn't me wandering around in the room, as I was then asleep by her side. After breakfast we debated whether we should ask the staff about any potential ghostly goings on and agreed that if we didn't it would be a lost opportunity.

The concierge who we spoke to at first elicited 'that look,' the one that suggests they know more than they are obliged to say, but after some light grilling, he was on the ropes. Alluding to a few incidents he had personally been involved in, I was assured there were others. He told us that on one occasion two guests who had stayed in our very suite, had to their shame only lasted half an hour before re-appearing at the desk. The gentleman in question, being Chinese and of a certain age remained stoic throughout as he asked for a change of room. The concierge somewhat perplexed at his request then enquired as to why they wanted a change, only to be told 'his wife did not like the presence.' Being the master of tact, he quickly made alternative arrangements, though at the time his eyebrows had raised slightly on hearing the gentlemen's request. What made him laugh the most though was the complainants stony face, which had remained impassive throughout as did his wife's, who stood discreetly behind with the suitcase.

Not so amusing was the fate of a young room attendant who was allegedly, 'persecuted,' by something while working. Whether mischievous or malignant, it was described as habitually pulling back the covers of freshly made beds. On other occasions it would leave an imprint on the bed where he assumed it had lain. Being the only key holder for those suites the possibility of it being a practical joke was quickly discounted. This experience proved very unpleasant and the poor chap then on the point of leaving, was relieved when it stopped abruptly some weeks later.

In 2019 I met an American psychic, then a first-time visitor to the city, who I took on a ghost tour. After a short while she indicated to me that she had mediumistic abilities. My natural cynicism immediately kicked in. Having met many people who purport to have psychic abilities over the years I generally take their statements with a pinch of salt, however on this occasion I would soon be sprinkling said condiment on some humble pie. On reaching the Witchery, she proceeded to tell me that the spirit of the dog which I had witnessed seven years previously, had been drawn to the suite because of an object in the bedroom. It was she said, a hat, which had belonged to its master while alive. She further stated that the hat can now be found sitting on a cabinet in the bedroom. I was hugely impressed, albeit somewhat taken aback, and confessed to her that during my stay I had taken some selfies while wearing the very garment!

The Witchery, so named, due to the inordinate number of unfortunates burned at the stake in the vicinity is without a doubt a haunted building. Guests have also reported, poltergeist activity in both rooms and in the restaurant, with chairs being moved on occasion. There has, or so I have been informed, been the occasional sighting of monks too which is understandable as to the proximity of the burnings. Perhaps they had oversaw some of those ghastly executions? Strangely, on the night we returned home my wife had a frightening experience after falling asleep on the settee. She woke with a terrified scream and once coherent explained to me that a male voice had spoken directly into her ear. The words were in Latin. Had something briefly attached itself to her after our visit?

But before we move on and speaking of witches, I must mention an article I came upon from a 2001 issue of the Telegraph. In it I was surprised to read the following headline: 'An exorcism was carried out yesterday by the head of the British White Witches to banish spirits from a local tourist attraction. Reading on I discovered that the exorcism had been held at the Edinburgh Dungeon. Hoping for something juicy I avidly read further though unfortunately the headline did not live up to its promise. Nevertheless, there was some amusement to be had when one 'spiritually' inclined member of staff intimated that perhaps one ride, prone to breaking down, was due to the resident spook. A slightly more prosaic comment came from their engineer who thought otherwise, in which he blamed faulty bolts.

Edinburgh Central Library
George IV Bridge

A short walk from the Witchery we soon reach George IV Bridge and on it the central library. I love libraries, not just because of what they contain, but for their atmosphere, the way they look and smell. I don't mean modern libraries, they hold no interest I mean vast airy rooms, furnished with dark oak containing labyrinthian basements crammed with dusty tomes. Places where time stands still are in my mind one of the spookiest settings for a story ever. Consider M R James's, masterful, 'The Tractate Middoth' for example. James was a man who realised the inherent creepiness to be found within their walls and his protagonists, simultaneously both scholars and busybodies, invariably found themselves in such places where their motives, lead to a salient lesson. They say, too much knowledge is a dangerous thing and in James's world, this was indeed true. There have of course been many reported incidents occurring within such buildings. They are a marriage made in ghostly heaven. But what of Edinburgh, so boastful of its haunted heritage, does Auld Reekie cut the mustard when it comes to libraries? Possibly, but although library ghosts appear a little thin on the ground in comparison to those in pubs and theatres, the quality of the following tale more than makes up for it. I was passed on this authentic and dare I say it, terrifying account quite recently and it took place in the bowels of Edinburgh's central library.

In the 1990's a local security guard named Colm was party to a genuinely disturbing encounter, which suggests the presence was capable of violent intent. The following is described in his own words. 'I am going back to approximately 1994, when I worked as a security guard for what used to be Securicor Guarding Services. Most of the time I supervised security down at the port of Leith but whenever there was a staff shortage, I would work in the city centre. Assignments included, banks, insurance buildings and libraries. I have always had an open mind when it comes to the paranormal and so when informed of ghosts and apparitions on these assignments, I would go out of my way to see them, this never happened in those times unfortunately.

One day the security officer that usually worked the night shift at the library was off ill, so I was asked to cover the shift. When the staff left at approximately 6pm, the guard would enter from the bridge and secure the door till around 8 in the morning. Our duties were to patrol the building every hour or two and swipe the clocking strips, so the client knew the patrol had taken place. At that time the reading room was on the bridge level, upstairs was the art departments, then if you walked through the reading room, behind the shelves at the rear, there was a door that led to a staircase. The staircase bought you down past another level, then down to an old well-secured door. This was underneath the bridge leading to the Cowgate. Being conscientious I patrolled the whole building. After checking the door at the bottom of the stairs I walked up to the first level which was through double doors.

14

This brought you into what was then an open plan office. After a few paces there was another door, which I presumed was a cupboard area. On this occasion I decided to check it out. The interior did not resemble the office, it looked like white painted stone walls. At the other end there looked to be an ancient door with a solid black metal rounded handle, so I thought I better make sure it was locked. The room itself resembled an old vault. In this room it looked as if it was only used as storage as on the right there was an old photo copier, a couple of old view finders and a sweeping brush and shovel propped against the wall. As soon as I tried the door, which was secure, I was punched in the stomach by an invisible force which knocked me into the middle of the room. As I hit the floor the light went off. I immediately knew this was paranormal and my fear was off the scale. I reached for the wall which had been on my left, but now on my right but before I could feel my way back to the office door my head felt a smashing pain which did not knock me unconscious but did put me in fear for my life. Eventually I found the door and worked my way up in the dark till I found the handle. I pushed and pulled but the door remained closed. I started saying a prayer which I had not done since primary school, after what seemed like forever the light came back on. The wooden sweeping brush was in two pieces, it was that which had been broken over my skull. When I opened the door, I realised there was no lock on the inner door and tried to run across the open plan room to get back to the double doors, but my legs were like lead. By the time I reached the stairs I managed through sheer will to climb on my hands and knees back up to the reading room. When I had composed myself, I phoned for a mobile supervisor though by the time he had arrived I had thrown up in the toilet. I was a perfectly fit

15

young man, did not drink that often and had never taken drugs. There was no doubt in my mind at the time, that this was a very dark and powerful entity. As soon as the supervisor arrived, he asked if I had patrolled the first floor as the regular guard refused, saying it was haunted. I walked off the job and have never set foot in the building again. About 10 years ago I came across a Scottish Paranormal Investigation group and on mentioning the library, one of the members said he knew someone who used to work there, and he remembered them saying the first floor was haunted. My blood ran cold again. Anybody wanting to investigate that area, I would suggest they take every precaution possible. I have had what I believe to be a few paranormal experiences in my life, but as far as physical harm goes this was by far the worse.'

Intrigued I contacted the library in hope of further details but was met with a dead end, it would appear the current staff have been spared. Good for them I thought, but bad for the reputation of such a venerable building. Afterwards, I concluded that the librarians, were probably overdue for a scare. Interestingly though, an older account from 1973, noted that members of staff at the time claimed to have seen the figure of a manacled Highland Chief in the lower floors beneath the arches. Why was he there remains open to question? Before we move on however, I would like to briefly mention nearby Merchant Street, which sits below the library building. A former employee of the club once situated there spoke recently of her experiences in the local paper. She was quoted as saying, 'I worked as a student on Merchant Street around twenty years ago. I absolutely hated going anywhere in the place alone. It just always had a horrible vibe. I also lost count how many times I saw a white silver shimmer appear then disappear from the mirrors on the dance floor.'

Heading back onto the High Street we now reach the Signet Library, on West Parliament Square, where Michele Catto passed on the following. 'I used to be a florist and I was often in the Signet Library setting up events. My experience happened while I was setting up for a wedding there. I remember on one occasion that the flowers were so lovely that I decided to take a photograph. It was then I noticed a man with long hair kept standing in front of me, while I tried to take the photograph. I then took several photos on my phone from different angles. When I checked them later, the man had appeared in nine of the images however my workmates said they saw nothing. What I saw was the back of the man, dressed in black clothing with a ponytail and he kept blocking my view.' Michelle went on to say that she had also heard the upper floor of the library is thought to be haunted. At the time of our conversation, I assumed by her description that the ghost was that of a contemporary figure, however I was assured that it was not.

No Business-like Snow Business: The Tron

B ack on the Royal Mile we now approach the spire of the Tron, the location of our next stop. This story until now unpublished, has all the classic tropes one would hope for in a creepy tale such as the lateness of the hour, the sighting of ghostly children and a satisfying if not altogether unsuspected denouement. There were also two credible witnesses, who both saw the same thing and to this day have sworn to its authenticity, which is reassuring. I don't suggest for a moment that people deliberately lie, but sometimes people misread situations, therefore some healthy scepticism is encouraged. Here's an example that occurred some years back, which on the face of it, sounded like a terrifying experience.

Some time ago I was given the opportunity to investigate the alleged paranormal activity that was plaguing a development in Aberdeen. The building a former Free Church of Scotland had in the 1980's been converted into a nightclub and subsequently sold on. Its usage was to remain the same, but all vestiges of its former décor was now gone leaving a dust filled building. I first heard about the location after reading an article in our local paper, The Press and Journal, affectionately known locally as the 'Pea and Ham.' Specializing in mainly local news from the Northeast its reports include, tale of vandalism, farming news with headlines such as 'Man Batters Fish' etc. However, that morning something more interesting nestled within its page as I gleefully perused the reported fate of a workman who, according to the article, had fled in terror from a 'haunted building.' The accompanying picture showing two terrified employees looking suitably downcast, had me unconvinced. Anyhow the long and short of it resulted in the story becoming a 'thing,' and though it's easy to be cynical, I put my money where my mouth is and asked if I could drop by. The owner seemed surprisingly amenable, so I duly arrived. According to the article the converted church was a hot bed of activity and phenomena included flickering lights, temperature drops and sightings of ghostly children, seen in recently taken photographs. The owner had also been informed that building now stood on the site of a cemetery which added a further layer. I could see where this was heading. Soon after I interviewed the workmen, at least those who had not fled, and they were happy to talk. They were a pragmatic bunch, indicating the state of the wiring as the cause for the flickering which indeed it was. As for the image of the phantom children? They were only dust particles, turned monstrous by an over-sensitive digital camera.

The following story however is different, having been witnessed by two people at the very same moment. Their account was passed onto me by an Ex- Edinburgh policeman or 'bobby,' as we prefer called Graham. During our conversation, he told me that in the early hours of one winter's morning in 1995 two police officers one male and one female, had returned from foot patrol, somewhat distressed. On arrival they recounted a terrifying experience they had on the High

Street. Naturally it resulted in mockery from their more cynical co-workers. Both frightened and frustrated at the lack of support, they confided in Graham, who had the decency to keep an open mind. Here is what he said: 'My friends were patrolling on the Royal Mile near Christmas time and the snow which had been falling heavily for some time, was now lying deeply. The scene was very picture postcard and being early in the morning there was not a single person on the street. When they arrived near the Royal McGregor (now closed but 154 High Street) they were stopped in their tracks by the sight of two young lads throwing snow in the air at the steps of the Tron church. The first thing they noticed was that both wore old fashioned clothes, shorts and caps. Secondly, they were smiling and appeared to be having a conversation between themselves, yet there was no sound. The atmosphere in the air was dull and flat as you would expect after snowfall. The boys glanced in the direction of the officers, who now were literally frozen in their tracks, before running around the corner down Niddry Street. My colleagues then bombed after them, wondering what the hell was going on, but when they turned the corner there was no sight of them. They were astonished to find that the boys had literally vanished, even though they were only seconds behind them. The officers on reflection, surmised there had been nowhere for them to go. The boys had left no footprints and the snow remained completely unscathed. Well, they got a fright of course and back at the station they proceeded to tell everyone. They had a hard time convincing people, most thought it was a joke. I knew it wasn't, they were genuinely scared even though most folk thought it was a windup.'

What a great story. A desolate street, deep snow and a satisfying conclusion, all on the ominous Royal Mile, what's not to like. Perhaps others have also seen the boys in the wee small hours? Maybe, as I suspect, the officers were just lucky to be in the right place the right time. Most people of course would blanche at the idea of such an encounter, but I would have loved it. Heading back up the High Street we now reach the City Chambers and below it possibly Edinburgh's most famous closes, Mary Kings.

Mary Kings Close

Mary Kings Close (a close being a lane or alley) is a historical tourist attraction run by 'Continuum' who run several similar venues. As with many other secret Edinburgh landmarks, it was largely forgotten until its rebirth as tourism grew, and like most of the surviving closes it has a tale to tell. Being synonymous as ground zero for the 1645 outbreak of the Black Death, its reputation is world famous and well documented, but does the amount of death associated with the area, mean its haunted?

This Edinburgh Close, much like most others, was narrow and overcrowded and to traverse its length would have been an experience, jostling for space among wandering livestock and dodging flying excrement only adding to the ambience. Despite this, the population which has been suggested numbered over two thousand in certain closes were not savages and would bawl out courteously to passers-by below, the word 'Gardyloo,' meaning watch the water. This delightful warning pre-empted the disposal of the contents of either a chamber pot, bucket or Chuntey and allowed the alert citizen below to react, the standard reply being 'haud yer hand.' Edinburgh wasn't known as Europe's dirtiest city for nothing, and it was possibly the greatest issue the city ever faced due in no small part to severe overcrowding. The buildings were at one point also very tall so one can imagine the damage which could be inflicted on the unwary below. In 1749 the Nastiness Act of Edinburgh was passed making it illegal to pollute the streets between the hours of seven and ten until the curfew was over. An old Edinburgh, tall tale, suggests that the plan was not wholly successful as the curfews end coincided with the closing time of taverns. One can picture the scenario, the milling drunks staggering home perhaps glancing above them as the windows open noisily, and they suggest the term being 'shit face' drunk derives from this unfortunate turn of events. It's probably unlikely as before the licensing acts ale houses often remained open if they were manned. Despite this, its grist to the mill to repeat the tale and provides a cheap laugh, and why not there's precious little to laugh at in the city's often bleak history. Why let the truth get in the way of a good story.

Although an unpleasant environment to live in something far more terrifying and insidious was about to come calling in the form of the Black Death, whose shadow swept across Europe in the year 1645. No strangers to the spectre of the bubonic plague due to a previous outbreak, the city was nevertheless ill prepared for the devastation that was to come. It was said that around a fifth of the population succumbed to its deadly embrace leaving only 60 able bodied men left to defend the city. Within a short time, the great brown rats, that first alighted on the docks of Leith now scuttled inwards spreading pestilence throughout the city.

Leith took the brunt of the first wave of the illness being next to the docks with near half the population succumbing before it crept inland. Why Mary Kings should be singled out as being the location of the first outbreak is open to question?

Perhaps it's the dreadful stories, that persist today of its poorly residents being sealed in? Perhaps it's the rumours their remains were butchered before being buried in mass graves? We will never really know, and as expected there is perhaps a degree of exaggeration being peddled today. At the onset of the outbreak, the area as far as we know was placed under quarantine, which was normal practice. The residents then had supplies passed to them while others were taken to the outskirts of the city to 'recuperate.' The residents of the close were also known to have been visited by Doctor George Rae, the plague doctor. One of the only men brave enough to venture in, he was a regular visitor, administrating to the sick, by applying a red-hot poker to the pus-filled buboes. Surprisingly many survived the ordeal as did he, protecting his flesh from deadly flea bites by wearing high leather boots, a thick cloak and terrifying 'bird mask.' Others weren't so lucky, and it is estimated around six hundred perished in the area. Today many existing plague pits remain in areas such as Bruntsfield, then Boroughmuir, and Morningside. Both described as being desirable areas in today's property market, I imagine prospective homeowners might be put off by the idea of a mound of corpses lurking below. Location, they say is everything, though I suspect local estate agents are neglectful of these facts when describing the locale. They also fail to mention the proliferation of ghosts that potentially reside in some of their properties, which is a pity as some might consider that a 'clincher.'

After the outbreak, life eventually returned to normal though the notion of the plague still lurking in the fabric of buildings was still a cause for apprehension, and so areas like Mary Kings Close were stigmatised for years. Properties were hard to let and a general air of reluctance to repopulate the area was palpable. But eventually the cities pragmatism won out, there was an acute housing shortage as always and soon enough new tenants drifted back.

Around forty years after the outbreak, the name Mary Kings Close suddenly came back into the public consciousness in an unexpected way with the publishing of Satan's Invisible world. The magnum opus of George Sinclair, a professor of moral philosophy at Glasgow University, the book is now recognised as providing supposed first-hand accounts of two of Edinburgh's most notorious hauntings that of Mary Kings Close and the Wizard of West Bow. Both stories give the modern reader an insight into the mindset of the times and the underlying themes portrayed suggest that the mental health of the protagonists helped create the mythology of today. The book is also lumbered with the most ungainly title ever being known fully as, 'Satan's invisible world discovered or a collection of modern relations providing evidently against the Sadducees and atheists of this present age, that devils, spirits, witches and apparitions from authentic records, attestations of famous witnesses and undoubted verity: to all which is added that marvellous history of major weir: with two revelations of apparitions at Edinburgh,' which is a very long title indeed!

Printed in 1685 locally it purports to be an account of true supernatural tales and is available to read or buy on kindle. Historically it is an interesting piece, describing in the same breath, both demons and spirits as being agents of Satan. On reading, it is perhaps a little unfair in its views towards spirits, but that was the mindset of the age in which it was written. Within its pages, the author describes the aftermath of the plague and subsequently the supernatural visitations that the new tenants endured. One story is regarded as being the template for everything ghostly that has since followed, the main witness being Thomas Coltheart. But the question remains, is it an accurate account of a haunting or something more fanciful? Most would agree it's the latter and the readers credulity is sorely tested as the story unfolds like a strange fever dream. The protagonists both devout Christians are also described frequently as resorting to 'fervent prayer' to rid themselves of their nightly visitations which speaks volumes. Below is a summary of events which were described in a chapter entitled, 'An apparition seen in a dwelling house in Mary Kings Close,' and it soon became apparent that the reputation of the house had preceded itself. On arrival one servant was said to have refused to enter the property, but the husband quickly, 'mansplains', away their fears. Soon after things take a turn for the worse when the tenants decide to take an afternoon nap their sanctity soon disturbed by the presence of an old man, whose disembodied head is then described as floating around the room like a balloon staring balefully at Mrs. Coltheart. Unsurprisingly she was said to have fainted. It was never mentioned how Mr. Coltheart took the news on awaking, but as bedtime approached, they lit a fire before retreating under the covers. Their peace however was short lived as the head re-appears, now accompanied by the apparition of a 'young child wearing a coat.' Terrified they begged God for help but despite the fervency of their prayers, 'a naked arm appears in the air from the elbow downward and the hands stretch out as when one-man salutes another.' Pulling the bed curtains around them to obscure the ghastly sight the poor couple could do little but cower in terror. After some time and convinced all was clear the husband eventually summoned the courage to peek out, only to see the arm, 'offer another salutation.' After much begging and entreating, the arm, we assume now exhausted by all the waving takes it upon itself to curl up in a nearby chair to sleep. The credulity of the reader is further stretched by almost comical descriptions that follow including that of a phantom dog and a cat. The couple in a fit of terror then flee only to find, 'the hall full of small little creatures, dancing prettily unto which no one could give a name as having never in nature seen the like.'

After the ghostly encounter, a patently ill Coltheart was then described as visiting Corstorfin (Corstorphine) on the outskirts of the city where preceding a sermon, he took refreshment at a public inn. Stepping to the door to 'ease nature,' he was then stricken 'with a vehement shivering and trembling in all his joynts.' Leaving rapidly the book then describes his approach to the outskirts of the city where a murder of crows began swooping and cawing ominously above his head. Rightly noting this as a portent of doom, the poor man passed within weeks. Ludicrous as the descriptions are we can only assume his illness may have played its part, but there was more to come.

The most intriguing part of the story is what transpired at his passing. Taken from an account by his employee a resident of nearby Tranent, he described the visitation from a cloudy figure on the day of Coltheart's death which appeared in his bedchamber. Recoiling in terror and drawing his sword before composing himself, he addressed it thus.

'Art thou my dear friend Thomas Coltheart? Art thou dead my friend? If thou hast any commission to me from almighty God, tell it me and shall be welcome.' Then the ghost according to his testimony, held up its hand three times and shaking it towards the startled witness vanished. The author then went on to say, 'this was done about the hours (as was guessed) of the agent's death,' thus making it one of the earliest recorded examples of a crisis apparition. Widely regarded as one of the most common of paranormal phenomena, the spirits purpose being that of messenger.

Since Coltheart's time the site remained populated until the early 20th century though surprisingly or unsurprisingly depending on your point of view, there were never any more recorded sightings. This changed dramatically in 1992 when interest in the close was reignited by a visiting psychic, Aiko Gibo. A well-known T.V personality in her native Japan, the medium claimed that while visiting Allan's Close (one of the rooms within the area) she felt a sudden wave of energy manifest itself. She then announced, 'I cannot enter this room, it is too strong, there is a child behind me her little hand is clutching my leg, I just cannot go into this room. She was separated from her parents, and she wants to go home and see her family, her desire haunts this place very strongly.'

Her vision of a small and forlorn girl called Annie was so overpowering that she was moved to gift her a doll, subsequently nicknamed 'Tartan Barbie.' She then placed the toy within Allan's Close, now known as Annie's room and soon after a legend was born. Afterwards the area swiftly became a shrine to the lonely spirit of Annie and since then visitors need little encouragement in leaving their own gifts. Today on entering Annie's room, the sight of hundreds of black soulless eyes can be a little disconcerting for those who find dolls creepy. In April 2019 'Tartan Barbie' vanished, and though I would like to say by supernatural means it was apparent an unscrupulous visitor had done the deed. To this day her whereabouts remain unknown despite a reward being offered. Like Annabel, Annie may want revenge and so perhaps in this instance we should wish the guilty party the best of luck!

Despite this, Annie is still believed to manifest her presence, and people to this day claim to have had their hands touched and sleeves tugged by the little spirit. To add further to this, I was told that some years ago a local photographer had apparently captured her image in which she was described as wearing a light-coloured gown. Could this be Annie, I hear you ask? We will probably never know as the image is still under wraps. Perhaps the owner is wary of ridicule? Either way it is potentially the only known photo of her to exist, but until it has been scrutinized......we can only guess.

Although Annie may be the most famous resident spirit there are, at least according to recent reports, many others. Before we move on, here are a few examples which describe phenomena ranging from poltergeist activity to unexplained scratching noises and sightings of a man in black clothing. There have also been sightings of a phantom calf (it was common for residents to keep livestock indoors) which begs the question, does it moo, or boo? Apologies. Either way interest in the close continues to grow and in a recent article former employee Laura Milne, was quoted as saying: 'I worked in Mary Kings Close for years and had to turn the light off myself at night, twice I had something unexplained happen, including a man follow me down an internal staircase.'

Visitors have also experienced unusual activity, take Laura Kerr who provided me with the following: 'A couple of years ago my family and I visited Mary Kings Close. In the room with the talking portraits my partner at the time screamed as something ran over his foot. There was no one nearby and I very much doubt a rat would have gotten that close to people. At the same time, I felt intensely cold and there was no draught that I could sense. When we stood up afterwards the temperature had returned to normal. Then later in Annie's room, my son was violently sick and started hyperventilating. My partner took him out as he was upset but I stayed with my other son to complete the tour. At the end of the tour when he looked back up the street (this is the area where the tour finishes) he clung to me like a limpet. He wouldn't say what was wrong other than he didn't like it. There was nothing or no one to be seen.' Another visitor in 2013 also reported a strange incident on entering Annie's room when the temperature plunged to an intolerably cold level. Strangely only the lower half of her body was affected, convincing her that the spirit of a small child stood in proximity. It was a disconcerting feeling made worse by then witnessing someone in near hysterics. What had been the cause she could not say, but witnesses observed, 'the manager having to attend to the incident.'

Other phenomena reported by visitors, have included children's voices being heard despite no children being on the tour and the sound of carousing echoing through the close. It goes without saying that noises from nearby hostelries were discounted. There have also been reports of the sound of scratching coming from a nearby chimney, where reportedly a young sweep once lost his life. More ominously an imposing cloaked figure has also been noted following a staff member in the process of locking up. Give me the prancing imps any day.

The Ghost of John Chiesley

Almost next door is the approximate location of another famous Edinburgh tale one that is both dark and gruesome. Well documented, and another example of an aged conker dropping from the tree of mistruth, it does however have a very interesting coda. Much has been said and written about the perpetrator and of his subsequent ghost. But how much of it is true? To find out let us return to the year 1689, where Edinburgh, then considerably smaller, is surrounded by Hamlets which would over time become part of the city. Dalry, near Haymarket was one such place and in it resided John Chiesley, a prominent businessman, a man of means and owner of Dalry house. Living there with his wife Margaret Nicholson, she bore him ten (or eleven children) depending on which account you read which no doubt put a strain on an already unhappy marriage. Chielsey, described as a bully with a violent temper agreed to a divorce which was a rare occurrence at the time, but baulked at the proposed alimony. The presiding advocate Sir George Lockhart who oversaw the proceedings, ruled in favour of Margaret, who was granted a hefty settlement of 1,700 merks equating to around £80,000 in today's currency. Always hot-headed, this insult pushed him over the edge and so he began to plot his revenge. With news of his intentions spreading quickly, Sir

George shrugged off the threats despite a letter being sent to him, which indicated, 'Chieslie, 'desir'd a speedy remedie' or 'he would attack him either in kirk or mercat.'

On 31st March 1689, on Easter Sunday, Sir George left the service at the High Kirk or New Church (St. Giles) as it was described. Unbeknownst to him his nemesis now followed having been seen lurking at the back of the church during the service. A report afterwards said. 'It was known that the villain was com'd from London till Sunday 31st, which day he came to the church, and offered money to the bedler for part of my Lord Castlehill's seat, just behind the President, who he designed to have murdered there; but not getting the seat, he would have none and walked up and down the church till the end of the sermon.'

Now in the company of Lord Castlehill and Daniel Lockhart, Sir George had reached the gate to his property where it was at that moment Chiesley made his move. Witnesses noted that Sir George Lockhart forgetting to mention something to his companion called back, and it was then Chielsey stepped forward. "I thought you were in London," remarked young Lockhart in surprise, "well I'm here now," retorted Chiesley and with that discharged his pistol into Sir George. The bullet described as going in beneath the right shoulder and out of the left pap, 'battered on the wall,' on its exit. Sir George immediately turned and looked his murderer in the face before collapsing. "Hold me Daniel, hold me," were his last words. In a vain attempt to save the stricken man he was then dragged inside and placed on the same bed as his now fainted wife, but it was hopeless. Outside, the murderer, described as making no attempt to flee appeared to revel in the spectacle and shouted aloud 'I have killed the judge, I have taught him justice.' He was at once set upon by the outraged crowd who held him firmly and on hearing that his victim had almost instantly expired declared with 'savage exultation' that, "he was not suited to doing things by half." He had sealed his fate though I suspect he would have flown had he known what was to come next. Rough hands now seized him, and he was borne off to the nearby prison where he was tortured mercilessly. Was he a paid assassin? Was he part of a political conspiracy? Who could commit such a crime for money? He was tortured for days to no avail. First, they used the Pinniken's which removed his fingernails. When this failed, the 'bootees,' were then applied. The 'bootees,' strips of wet leather, were wrapped tightly around the poor devils' lower legs and then slowly dried by suspending the leg above a flame resulting in his lower limbs being crushed horribly. On execution day the now grievously injured landowner was brought at last before the baying mob where his right hand was struck off at the wrist, this being the hand that had fired the murder weapon and then at last he was hung. It's fair to say that people enjoyed the spectacle of an execution and would need little encouragement in participating. Afterwards his body was then transported to Drumsheaugh and placed inside a gibbet where the sight of its slow decomposition would serve as a warning to others. To spare his suffering wife and children further horrors, the body however soon vanished. But to where? The question would remain unanswered for nearly two hundred years.

Soon after alleged sightings of Chiesley's crippled shade were witnessed in Dalry, accosting unwary travellers. His bloodied face and grasping arm soon became the thing of legend and thus was born, 'Johnny one-arm.' Whether the sightings were real or not remains contentious for there are no actual witnesses that I am aware off. Nevertheless, it was enough to stop people travelling through the lonely woods and lanes near his former home. The haunting, if the story is to be believed, continued until 1965 when allegedly his skeletal remains were discovered by two workmen. His subsequent burial then put paid to his night-time ramblings. It's a great story, but somewhat unlikely given there were no headlines detailing their find in that year. Still, hoping to add flesh to the bones as it were, I was heartened to chance upon a letter which suggested his remains were discovered much earlier. The letter dated 15th January 1829, written to the secretary of an antiquarian society was from none other than Sir Walter Scott. It revealed the following.

'I return the curious and particular account of Sir George Lockhart's murder by Chieslie of Dalry. It is worthy of antiquarian annotation, that Chieslie was appointed to the gibbet, somewhere about Drumsheaugh. As he was a family man, the gibbet was privately cut down and the body carried off. A good many years since some alterations were in the house of Dalry, when on enlarging a closet or cellar in the lower story, a discovery was made of a skeleton, and some fragments of iron, which were generally supposed to be the bones of the murderer. His friends had probably concealed them when they were taken down from the gibbet, and as no opportunity had occurred for removing them before their existence was forgotten. I was told of the circumstances by Mr James Walker, then my brother in office, and proprietor of Dalry. I do not however recollect the exact circumstances, but I daresay Frances Walker Drummond, can supply my deficiency of memory.' If this is true, his remains were found much earlier than has been oft quoted.

Despite his burial, certain contemporary accounts still describe his figure haunting the closes nearest to the execution site, but I have found no evidence to support this. Like many things in the modern world contemporary ghost stories often pale in comparison from those in the past, and this one is no exception and having gone from a limping bloodied figure to a mere pushing hand is something of a come down. Modern storytellers have even suggested that the 'ghost,' which allegedly haunts the closes of the High Street today is that of the hand/arm that was so carelessly disposed of after the execution. There are even some who claim to have been pushed by those very demonic digits but in all fairness the combination of uneven steps and alcohol is likely the culprit. To illustrate this please see below.

While on my tour around three years ago, in Advocates Close, as near as one can get to the original murder site of Old Bank Close. As I recounted the story you have just read, the crowd was alerted by a sudden cry from behind. We turned on mass only to observe a man tumbling down the steps in front of our startled eyes. They are an impressive set of steps for those unfamiliar with them, and the spectacle reminded me of a low rent version of the Exorcist's finale. The crowd then surged backwards pressing themselves against the opposing wall while those of a more nervous disposition screamed. At the foot of the stairs now lay a prone figure who after staggering to his feet bounced and stumbled on his way. Terror quickly turned to laughter as the spirits involved, turned out to be those of the whisky variety, his breath leaving a wonderful residue in the air. After the initial shock much merriment ensued, no doubt bolstered by the mundane denouement. The best part was, that once the group had recovered their composure someone asked me if I had paid him to do it. This has provided me with a great anecdote ever since.

But things were to change when in May of 2019 a group of nine ladies from Glasgow attended my tour. We stood in Advocates Close where I recounted the tale and as the story unfolded, I noticed one of the ladies looked a little surprised. Afterwards she stepped forward and intimated that she knew Dalry House well having visited it in the 1960's This is what she said:

'My best friend and her husband rented a flat in Dalry House for around ten years. It was their first flat together, being newly married, and it was on the top floor of the building. She told me on many occasions what they had experienced while living there. It was described as haunted, and the figure of a man was often seen in the flat wandering about at the foot of their bed or sometimes just standing in the dark watching. This was both late at night and early in the morning. She said to me that they saw him frequently. Her husband also saw the figure of a man walk straight through a wall once while lying in bed. When the figure got to the other end of the room it just walked through that one as well. This happened twice I was told. Sometimes they would be lying in bed at night and feel a presence in the room or wake up as if they had a nightmare. They would cautiously glance over and the same man would be standing at the foot of their bed. They used to pull the covers up around them and just wait till he went.'

I was of course delighted to hear about their experiences, but questioned why on earth would someone want to stay in a building for ten years when it was so obviously haunted? It was because of the 'cheap rent,' I was told. Of course, whether the spirit was that of its most infamous inhabitant remains unanswered, but either way I was hugely impressed. Still standing today, the house has now been converted into luxury flats, and very nice they are too. With prices starting at offers over an eye watering £500,000, they offer all mod cons and potentially a free ghost which might be the clincher for some. It has had a long and illustrious history and was once used as a teacher training college where the venerable Scottish actor Alistair Sim once taught.

It was also thought to have been used by King Charles I as a love nest and antiquarian photos suggest it was a characterful house containing all manner of architectural gems, including a painted ceiling. I surprised some time later to find out it had also been a community space and on visiting the central library to find out more was kindly given a book of articles relating to this. The Gorgie / Dalry Gazette of 1989 was my first port of call and I read avidly several reports relating to its alleged haunting. This was music to my ears, well it least my eyes. The first interview I read was from Sam, a housekeeper. In the article she appeared more than happy to talk about her experiences which centred around the 1st floor, which she preferred to avoid at night. Reported phenomena included the lift operating of its own volition, water being turned off at the mains and lights flicking on and off randomly. One could of course put some of these incidents down to faulty mechanisms, but what of chairs being stacked and unstacked, a phenomenon reported on more than one occasion? Even more compelling was the sight of 'shadow figures being seen to 'rest in armchairs.' She went on to state that on one occasion she was convinced that the figure of a woman had passed her on stairs, leaving behind the pungent smell of perfume. Could this have been the king's former lover? In the hope of obtaining answers, 'The White Feather Centre,' was contacted and a group of psychics visited soon after. After around fifteen minutes they claimed to have encountered two hitherto unknown spirits, that of a former housekeeper and a stable boy respectively.

It was big news and soon after a succession of first-hand accounts from both former pupils and workers were received. This of course vindicated the current workers whose stories had no doubt been mocked and for a while there was a resurgence of interest in the building. For example, a former cleaner Mrs. Fraser described how on occasion her hoover would start on its own. She further stated that a former caretaker had left the post due to creepy encounters including a locked door suddenly swinging open. In another issue, a Mrs. Cook recalled an incident earlier last century when her mum worked there from 1903 till 1906. At that time, it was used as a lady's college. She recalled being told her father used to visit his future wife while courting so they could have lunch together. She then stated that one day while her father was waiting in the hall, he 'heard a rustling sound and saw a grey vision.' Creepy stuff and I would have loved to have found out more.

Reading further another article later revealed that a second mysterious burial had also been uncovered late last century when unwitting workmen uncovered a headless corpse beneath an old summer house. If this is true, perhaps it too may have some bearing on the proceedings. Whether the current crop of owners have had any experiences remains open, but this new information at least adds a little weight to it being potentially haunted. And why not, a building of its stature deserves to be?

As a footnote, I read with interest the fate of Chiesley's daughter Rachael, who according to accounts inherited her father's fiery temperament. Marrying a successful Scottish Lawyer, Lord Grange, she was afforded the title of 'Lady' though some argued she was a lady by title alone. Known for her wild behaviour, the citizens of the Royal Mile were frequently treated to her increasingly bizarre behaviour including threatening to run through the streets of Edinburgh naked. A rash idea considering our weather. Described as remonstrating with her husband in both church and street, Lord Grange was known to have hidden (with one of his sons) in a nearby tavern to escape her wrath. History always paints a one-sided picture which was proven, when her husband, the stoic victim suddenly revealed a darker side by orchestrating her kidnap from the streets of Edinburgh. She was then driven north where unbelievably she spent the rest of her life being moved from island to island off the West Coast of Scotland. Skye, St Kilda and others, all became home to her at various times and despite being given sustenance and shelter all communication with the outside world was stopped. Described as spending her days wandering the windswept shores, escape was out of the question, the mainland tantalizingly close yet impossible to reach because of the treacherous waters. Her captors, Gaelic speaking Highlanders could not or would not communicate and being handsomely bribed followed their orders to the letter. There was no overt cruelty, yet she was forced to live in the most rudimentary conditions, residing in both stone huts and caves. Food was meagre, yet whiskey was relatively plentiful, and she drank freely as she did in her previous life. Strange as it seems, no serious attempt was ever made to secure her return despite twice sneaking letters to her lawyer in Edinburgh, through a sympathetic minister. Her husband remained obstinately silent over the matter, his money and power buying loyalty. She ended her days in the same enforced exile and never once set foot back in Edinburgh. Never seen as a sympathetic character, she frequently reminded her husband of whose daughter she was, perhaps no idle threat.

The Quaker meeting House:
Major Weir

E nough to cause anyone to quake, this house was once
described as one of the most haunted in Edinburgh
due to a previous incumbent the 'Wizard of West
Bow.' No relation to Mr. Potter, in case you wondered. Major
weir, the wizard himself, was a retired soldier and a man of
great piety and both he and his sister Jane or Grizel as she was
sometimes known frequented church. Of course, attending
church does not make you above suspicion, but in those days
it certainly looked good. One day after a period of unspecified
illness Wier announced to the startled congregation that had
made a pact with the devil. According to his testimony this
arrangement had been long standing and in doing so he had
enjoyed carnal knowledge, as opposed to carnal ignorance,
with livestock from the nearby Grassmarket. Their expressions must have been priceless. News spread quickly and the
public unable to comprehend his admissions were then dealt
a further blow when he declared that both he and his sister
had lived as man and wife for years. This revelation, as hard
as it was to believe resulted in their incarceration.

A description of the preceding events was noted in the
aforementioned George Sinclair's, 'Satan's Invisible world.'

Described as a 'choice collection on modern relations, proving evidently against the saducees and atheists of this presents age, that there are devils, spirits, witches and apparitions from authentic records.' The book claimed to be actual eyewitness accounts of the events leading up to Weir's execution and subsequently his sisters and as you have already seen it also includes the history of Mary Kings'! Initially no one believed his revelations but soon his insistence became deafening. A chance for redemption was offered on the understanding that he renounced evil, but he refused and was quoted as saying, 'Let me be, I will not. I lived as a beast and must die as a beast.' His sister joined him in prison soon after. Was he ill, perhaps suffering from dementia? We will never know, but their rabid confessions ended in a guilty verdict. Perhaps the devil was literally in the detail but for their sins both were executed, Weir at Carlton hill where his famed staff joined him in the flames. Eyewitnesses at the time claimed it writhed in fury as the fire took hold, taking an inordinate amount of time to burn. Soon after poor Jane/ Grizel met an equally sorry end and on reading details of the trial, the truth becomes clearer. Having forced himself upon his sister and sexually assaulted her for years we can only assume the trauma involved, and the subsequent mental state which led to her confession. To say Weir was deeply flawed would be a gross understatement and he would have, I suggest, have made a greater role model for Mr. Hyde than our old friend Deacon Brodie.

A contemporary account stated. 'His sister asked where his staff was, for it seems she knew that his strength lay therein. He told her it was burnt with him, whereupon notwithstanding of her age, she nimbly, and in furious rage fell on her knees uttering words horrible to remember, "O Sir I know he is with the devils, for with them he lived." During a further confession, 'She avouched that from being sixteen years of age, to her fiftieth, her brother had the incestuous use of her body, and then loathed her for her age.' She made no attempt to save herself and on reading it appears she had given up. Did they really have Satanic beliefs or was it, hysteria, guilt, illness that ultimately sealed their fate? Insane rumours then began to circulate including on which suggested Grizel was in possession of a bewitched spinning wheel that produced endless yarn, much like this story. Another suggested their vacant home now derelict and boarded was a 'house of horrors,' and people pondered on what diabolical practices had taken place there. It was a magnet for the curious and strange lights were said to issue from the locked building. Soon after a phantom coach pulled by demonic steeds swept down Victoria Street, or so it was said, bearing the doomed soul of Wier. This of course is fantasy and even the naivest guide, would blanche at its telling. Saying that, even the great Walter Scott himself was not above a little rumour mongering remarking upon the very house when he said, 'bold indeed was the urchin who approached the gloomy house in West Bow with the risk of seeing Major Wier's enchanted staff parading the desolate apartments or hearing the hum of the necromantic wheel of his sister Grizel.'

The house despite its reputation did eventually gain new tenants, though apparently after much persuasion and if the account is to be believed they still hold the record for the world's shortest tenancy, lasting exactly one day. Another tenant, an eccentric who shunned company inadvertently fanned the flames further. Described as a night owl his midnight wanderings soon came to the attention of his neighbours. It was the sight of his lone candle glowing faintly behind the heavily curtained windows that conjured up all sorts of devilish images, or so they say.

Today part of the original structure survives having thought to have been demolished. Now incorporated into the current the Quaker House, it is hidden in the lower reaches of the building, and it comes as no surprise that Weir allegedly still makes the odd appearance. Apparently witnessed in recent times near a photocopier in the office, the machine that is, not the person his visitations are best described as infrequent. In respect of this I did try to ascertain if there had been any recent notable appearances but drew a blank.

Interestingly though a recent conversation with a spiritualist suggested the streets reputation for being haunted is not unfounded as they have conducted several blessings (an exorcism for a building if you like) there. I was not given further details, other than that there have been five investigations in recent years. Of those five around two appeared to potentially be of supernatural origin while the other three appeared to be a case of mistaken identity. Despite its reputation, I must conclude that the jury is out on whether this can rightfully be described as a haunted location.

In conclusion, I used to tell the story of Major Weir on my ghost tours, but found that people were not very enamoured with the tale, perhaps it was the subject of incest or maybe the bestiality aspect that was the turn off? Maybe it was the lack of any actual ghost encounters that had soured the mood? On my very last airing of the tale, a young Malaysian on my tour announced to the group that while listening to the story he had become aware of a man watching us from an upper window in the building. He then claimed he was psychic, and at that the group took a collective step backwards. I began to peer hesitantly upwards, but I could see nothing but the blankly staring glass. Despite this he remained insistent and the group whether they believed him or not seemed glad to move on. Prior to our departure however he casually mentioned, that in the future I should, "watch out for trees". I often wish he hadn't as I love trees and the thought of being clobbered by a falling branch, to this day, ironically haunts me. I found out some months later that co-incidentally my two colleagues, John and Alvaro once shared a flat next to 'The House of Horrors.' A recent conversation revealed that one evening while gaming, John was alerted by the sound of footsteps overhead from the attic. His flat being the only property to have access discounted the noise coming from his neighbours and so fetching a ladder he peered tentatively into the attic. It was of course empty and so returned to his gaming, only to hear the footsteps start up again. Damn elusive ghosts!

Greyfriars Cemetery

A short walk from West Bow and we reach the Grassmarket where around the corner lies Greyfriars cemetery. You can't beat a good graveyard and Edinburgh is blessed with more than its fair share including Calton, Cannongate and Warriston to name but a few. They all come with their own legends and stories, but the most notorious is Greyfriars. With an atmosphere you could cut with a knife on occasion, it is by all accounts a genuinely haunted location being home to a violent entity known as the Mackenzie poltergeist. Spirits witnessed within the cemetery walls include that of a figure in black wearing a quaker type hat, a young girl in white and forlorn ragged figures witnessed at the nearby Covenanters prison. The stories have been well documented and are plentiful and I am particularly pleased to have been able to add further to this ever-growing list. Whether it is the nauseating smell of corruption that assails the nostrils of the unwary or the random bites and scratches that appear on visitors, the sheer number of accounts are impressive. Compared to other supposed haunted locations this one has substance. It is no idle boast to suggest that many regard it as Europe's most haunted cemetery.

Before we continue let's take a quick look at the supposed entity, at least when in human form. George Mackenzie of

Rosehaugh, born in Dundee in 1636 and rose to the rank of Lord Advocate before being knighted. Power and position corrupt, and he is a case in point. Of course, it's too simplistic to sight this as the sole reason for his transformation into one of the most despised men in the land. Suffice to say he was a wicked spiteful man, whose hatred of the Covenanters knew no bounds. The Scottish Presbyterians who gathered in Greyfriars cemetery to sign the National Covenant 1638 had no idea of the ramifications that would follow, and the part Mackenzie would play. Initially opposed to Charles I and his interference in the Church of Scotland, the signing of the Covenant led to the bishop's wars and ultimately the English civil war. Charles I was then turned over to the government forces by his Scots captors, something his son wouldn't forget. The son in question, Charles II ironically signed the very document himself, to gain support of the Scots. This earned him the title 'King of Scots,' though afterwards he reneged on the deal. The persecutions which followed were brutal and the now captured Covenanters were held in a large field at the back of Greyfriars. It has since been described as the world's first concentration camp, though it is now known as the Covenanters prison. The captives, those who didn't succumb to the harsh conditions or swear allegiance to the king, were then executed at the Grassmarket. It is thought, the remainder were then transported for a life of slavery, although their ship sank off the coast of Orkney. A mere handful survived out of the estimated one thousand two hundred prisoners. It goes without saying that their tormented souls, aimless and transparent have since been witnessed within the confines of the prison.

As someone who has led hundreds of tours, I must confess that on most occasions I have not seen anything untoward but there are however exceptions, and it was on one of those nights that the following happened. On that evening it was dark, the lights in the Kirk long extinguished, and the lamp at the main gate in need of repair. Even George Heriots school, if I remember correctly wasn't playing ball that night and sat there in shadow. On that occasion I stood within the gates allowing my eyes to get accustomed to the dark. Leading my group along the side of the church towards an intersection near the Flodden Wall, I suddenly became aware of a figure in white drifting long the path directly ahead. I can only describe it as if it were someone wearing a white sheet over them but having no discernible features, and my heart literally jumped within my chest. To my relief, at the intersection I was met with nothing. I have no idea who or what it was however it is an image that has stuck with me ever since. Absurdly it looked like someone literally wearing a sheet over their head, like a child's Halloween costume, minus the eye holes of course. Afterwards my rational side came to the fore, and I argued that perhaps I was tired and had been mistaken.

There have also been an inordinate number of intriguing photographs taken in the vicinity of Mackenzie's mausoleum, though typically most capture nothing more than dust orbs. There have of course been exceptions, the most arresting being a luminous snake like image which wove itself between the participants. The photographer was a young lady from Ireland who then proceeded to show her excited tour mates the image which led to the quickest exit ever. I was glad on that occasion that they had tipped me first.

In 2020, I had a personal experience in the vicinity of the mausoleum which I would like to share with you. On that occasion the weather was glorious and Greyfriars was busy with folk enjoying their 'designated' hours exercise. I had decided during lockdown to set up a YouTube channel, nothing earth shattering just me telling a few ghost stories which my wife had volunteered to film. We then wondered around Edinburgh's most haunted hotspots. Eventually we ended up in Greyfriars where we opted to film at the Covenanters prison. Now standing at the prison the filming was interrupted as Carol screamed and jumped behind me. I stupidly thought she had been stung by a wasp however, it was nothing so mundane. After the initial shock, she went on to described being grabbed firmly on the shoulder by an invisible entity. She stated afterwards it was like a friend had crept up behind her and placed a hand firmly on her shoulder. Standing with our eyes darting frantically we were relieved when nothing else occurred and deeming it safe to leave we headed towards the gate. Once outside we debated whether to continue filming and after a few minutes of pontification we did. Once inside we then met our friend Kenny who at the time had been walking his dog. He seemed a little taken aback when we described the incident which he had witnessed from afar. Since then, my wife has shown great reluctance in returning.

Not long after I was interested to read a recent article in the local paper in which around 200 plus locals responded to the question do you believe in ghosts? If I'm honest I do find these polls a little discouraging and concluded on reading, that the public should never be asked anything. There were of course some intelligent responses, but generally forums of this type are designed for mouth breathers to vent. On this occasion like most others, it was a mixed bag. Contributions ranged from genuinely interested parties to cynical pie munchers. The standard, 'ghosts, they dinnae exist, it's a load a shite,' was to the fore as expected, however those were interspersed with some great accounts some of which I have taken the liberty of detailing below. The following incident was related by an Edinburgh resident, who as a child was taken to Greyfriars on a school trip.

These are his own words. 'I remember going there in primary school as a kid and I kept looking at all the people standing behind us in costume but being told by the teacher there was nobody there and to pay attention to the guide. I am still convinced people were there.' A school trip to a graveyard is always a winner. But who were they? Did he witness a timeslip, in which some ancient tragedy plays out giving the right atmosphere? We cannot say, yet this intriguing phenomenon is not that uncommon. I have spoken to many witnesses who have experienced being 'out of place' over the years, and most of the experiences have involved sightings of larger groups. For example, someone visiting a museum I used to work at walked into what she described as a prayer meeting once and described seeing multiple figures. She left hurriedly and on returning with an attendant found the room to be empty, which is what I have expected in a good ghost story. Another interviewee, this time from Aberdeen described once taking a short cut to meet some friends, soon finding himself in a similar scenario. On that occasion he literally stumbled across a gathering of 2nd World War soldiers. Bolting from the scene he eventually persuaded his friends to return only to find the area once again deserted. His friends of course did not believe him despite his entreaties, quite a common occurrence it would seem, though he did appear consoled that I did. Is it down to timing, an anniversary perhaps? Is it because of the geological conditions in the area where the event occurred? These are perfectly reasonable assumptions in a subject so nebulas.

Author Jan Andrew Henderson is possibly better placed than most to have his say having ran the successful 'City of the Dead Tours,' for years. His company are the sole keyholders to the gated area where most of the activity has taken place and as an author he has written extensively on the subject. Recently I spoke to the company manager, Jamie Corstorphine for further details. Luckily his office sits within the confines of the Kirkyard and was once used for the storage of dead bodies which I suppose is apt. He has thankfully avoided any personal experiences so far but retains an open mind on the subject and has a wealth of knowledge on the area. Percentage wise only a small amount of people it would seem are blessed with an experience, like going whale watching or trying to catch the Northern Lights I suppose. Even Jan who is openly sceptical about the afterlife, was quoted as saying, 'If this is not a genuine supernatural case then I don't think there is such a thing,' Given the amount of phenomena we are about to look at proves that even a sceptic can hedge their bets on occasion. Stranger still is that the poltergeist, if that what it is, shows none of the behavioural characteristics of a traditional noisy ghost eschewing short term activity for a long campaign. There is also a school of thought that suggests the poltergeists' activities are potentially active over multiple locations. Diverse properties such as the Radisson Hotel on Niddry Street, near the site of Mackenzie's former home, and nearby Candlemaker Row are both thought to share similar phenomena which have included sporadic fires. In recent years one such fire caused significant damage to the hotel which raised a several questions as to the cause. The jury remains out.

There are of course many theories concerning the nature of the hauntings. Some say it a possible discarnate entity, perhaps demonic, which haunts the area. Others suggest that perhaps it is a poltergeist just not following the rules? Scientists keen to disprove the notion of hauntings being paranormal recently had some guinea pigs, human ones that is, take part in a recent study. In the study a volunteer group were taken to an undisclosed location. Before they arrived, one group was told the area was haunted while the other was given no information. Both groups were then asked to look around the location and record any feelings or sensations they might have had. As you can imagine some who had prior knowledge recorded a feeling of unease. Sceptics must have been rubbing the hands with glee; however, their triumph was short lived as the results proved inconsistent. A similar study at Hampton Court also produced mixed results. Despite this, there was still enough data to suggest that those primed before visiting took with them a healthy dose of subliminal anticipation. It's a given that anyone with a passing interest in the subject secretly hopes to see something out of the ordinary, and no doubt feel a tinge of disappointment when they don't. Regarding those who may have experienced the poltergeist, no amount scientific explanation can sway their opinions. Whether it is imagination or something supernatural will depend on your perspective, but what cannot be denied is that visitors to the cemetery continue to have experiences, as the following from a visitor from London demonstrates. 'I felt light-headed, I had pins and needles and didn't feel like my hands were mine. I kept fighting it but felt nauseous and had palpitations. That's when I got hit on the head. It was inside like my brain had been slapped. I managed to get out but couldn't stop crying. It was like grieving.'

Another tourist, this time from York, wrote. 'When I was standing in the tomb, something soft like cotton wool was touching my neck and cheek. There was nobody doing this to me. The next day I woke up with a black eye and scratches on my face and neck.' Personally, I think I prefer my ghosts a little cosier, though the debate over what actual 'haunts,' the cemetery continues. Mercifully though on most of my tours very little ghostliness happens, which suits me well. I am not against the idea, it's just I prefer to be spooked on my own, rather than being responsible for others. When it has happened, the results so far have been low key. For example, on a recent tour a gentleman from Hull, very politely informed me that his arm had been pinched while standing at the gates of the prison. He took it very well I have to say, but he did look rather pale. His wife assured me he wouldn't lie, and I had no reason to doubt him. I made sure I escorted him to the gate where he seemed relieved though afterwards, I regretted not asking for his details. Perhaps like most 'victims,' he may have sustained an injury. Not long after a couple from Somerset related a very similar set of circumstances, describing how her husband found numerous scratches on his back on returning home from a tour. I tried to picture their conversation that evening though I expect it was a little fraught. They seemed genuine and though I had no reason to doubt them I almost asked him to show me his back, then realizing he barely knew me I resisted the urge. Then there was the woman who recently had her hair tugged…. the list goes on.

A medium once told me that despite what people think, graveyards are possibly the least haunted places on earth, which at the time I found perplexing. It was his belief that given the choice of a dingy graveyard or paradise, which would be the most tempting? I suspected the latter, to which he concurred. Today we are left wondering if the resident ghosts are mere recordings in the fabric of the place, slowly fading over time? The graveyard of course always had a reputation, but it wasn't until the 1990's that the name Mackenzie became synonymous with the haunting and he has in the last twenty or so years become its resident bogeyman. They say that the reason his angry spirit now haunts the area is because of two well documented break-ins, unlikely but it does makes good copy. Here is what happened.

Some years ago, a homeless man allegedly broke into the last resting place of George Mackenzie to seek shelter for the night. He entered by a large air vent at the rear of the mausoleum and not content to bed down was thought to have gone below into the burial chamber for a poke around which is accessed by a metal grill. What happened next is open to interpretation as there are several different versions of the story circulating, but the most likely scenario is that he slipped on the uneven surface of the floor landing on the remains of a prior burial. The remains are thought to belong to the original incumbents the Forrester family who suffered the indignity of being ousted from the spot by Mackenzie. The man, it is assumed, then grabbed onto a nearby coffin before accidentally snapping off a portion as he fell. According to reports he then vacated the building noisily before disappearing from the history books. The subsequent search then exposed his blunderings and as previous reports suggest, the rumours of grave robbing was born. There are even more outlandish stories that suggest, the floor of the mausoleum caved in beneath his feet sending him plunging into a plague pit, which seems implausible. Flying in terror it was then reported that he knocked down a night watchman, a dog walker or in one instance some passing Goths. Neither of these scenarios took place, which some might argue is unfortunate.

Despite this, the ancient tradition of knocking on the door of Mackenzie's tomb persists. Considered a rite of passage, local lads were known to dare each other to approach the last resting place of, 'Bluidy Mackenzie,' where a sharp knock would no doubt be followed by a sharp exit. The areas reputation is nothing new. In Cassell's 'Old and New Edinburgh,' records show that local kids in the 19th century believed McKenzie's ghost was real, a case of one's reputation preceding itself. There was even a rhyme which you were obliged to say through the keyhole, before knocking: 'Bluidy MacKenzie come out if ye daur, lift the sneck and draw the bar.' The author Robert Louis Stevenson even got in on the act, penning the following: 'when a man's soul is certainly in hell his body will scarce lie quiet in a tomb sometime or other the door must open, and the reprobate come forth in the abhorred garments of the grave.' Beautifully put.

Speaking of which, around 18 years ago something did come forth, though not by its own volition, and even Edinburgh, well versed in dark history drew breath as the magnitude of the act was revealed. The incident, now as ingrained in Edinburgh lore as Mackenzie's antics, involved some local teenagers, who on breaking into the mausoleum removed the head of one of the corpses using a penknife. The eldest of the group then put his fist into its neck and, 'talked to it like a puppet,' Later caught returning to the scene of the crime, he then wrapped his 'souvenir' in a blanket with the intention of showing one of the girls in his company. She was unimpressed, and her following screams caught the attention of a passing tour who witnessed the whole debacle. Participating in a ghost tour, I suspect on that evening they got more than their money's worth. Ironically the group was being led by the keyholder to the Covenanters Prison, Jan Andrew

Henderson who in the ensuing melee had to detain the lad till the authorities arrived. The mummified head, which was thought to be that of Mackenzie's daughter was then discreetly rescued but not before it had been unceremoniously booted across the grass in front of the startled onlookers. Narrowly avoiding jail, a three-year probation was ordered by the judge who described the case as, 'gruesome and revolting.' Both were charged under ancient legislation used to prosecute graverobbers, the charge being the 'violation of a sepulchre.' The poltergeist attacks preceding the break in, were of course blamed on his angry spirit. Whether this is true or not remains open to question though since that day peculiar incidents periodically occur.

There have of course been several investigations into the area, and one conducted by 'Strange Phenomena Investigation' (SPI) grabbed my attention, their report refreshingly underplaying what transpired. They undertook two visits the first in 2000 and were given access by the city council to the area. Finding little evidence, they found out afterwards they had been taken to the wrong mausoleum. The council no doubt ashamed then arranged for a further visit. On arrival the mediums sensed a negative force within the vault. They described it as only being present in one part of the area, next to the wall. Using electronic sensors, they found that the electromagnetic readings spiked at the same spot. It was unusual. With little else achieved the first investigation ended, it was a little underwhelming. The second visit took place soon afterwards and was bolstered by being featured on the BBC's 'Heaven and Earth' program, therefore hopes were higher. This time, the team was joined by presenter Toyah Wilcox, who no doubt remarked afterwards, 'it's a mystery,' sorry I couldn't resist. This time on entering the adjacent burial chamber to the famed 'Black Mausoleum,' things proved different. Once inside the mediums described feelings of terrible nausea and faintness, however the crew felt nothing. They then claimed to sense a young boy standing near a doorway. More disturbingly, an 'appalling smell, like rotten meat, filth and offal,' permeated the vault. They then went on to describe something not being right about the area, a feeling of death and corruption and were convinced that something had taken place within its four walls. They sensed it was an area used for a black mass or another satanic ritual and described whatever it was, was a 'lower astral entity.'

There have of course been other peculiar phenomena ascribed to area, including that of a proliferation of dead animals found near the mausoleum. My colleague Alvaro, bore witness to this himself some years ago. A native of a small village in Spain, he mentioned that in the area where he was from, people used the local cemetery almost like a park and it was not unusual for residents to drink and play guitar in such surroundings. Carrying on with this tradition he soon found himself along with two companions having a late tipple in the cemetery. It was as he described, a very low-key affair and for entertainment began to tell them the story of the Mackenzie poltergeist. Sitting near the mausoleum he described why the gates were always kept locked and what people had encountered there. Delighted by his audience's rapt attention he continued and on mentioning Mackenzie's name, a dead bird or at least part of one suddenly dropped from an overhanging tree. It was a sobering moment, its carcass repulsing those present. Could it just have been a bizarre co-incidence? Perhaps, but they took it as a signal to leave. Sometime later, this time in the company of friends Andrea and Maria, another unsettling experience occurred in the same location. As before they had sat chatting and after a few beers Andrea took it upon herself to investigate the area. When she failed to return, they found their terrified and tearful friend sitting in a nearby doorway. On questioning she described seeing a young girl dressed in white and out of curiosity had followed her. The girl, keeping a little distance ahead then stopped near a headstone before vanishing. After some time, Andrea took them to the spot where she had seen the girl, but on arrival all was still. When I asked Alvaro if he remembered the name on the headstone, he replied, Elizabeth.

As I've discovered probably around 90% of sightings within the cemetery are attributed to Mackenzie, though I am pleased to note he doesn't always have the monopoly. Take for example the following report. Recently featured in a local forum, Barbara described to me her visit to the Covenanters prison. 'I saw a man dressed in black wandering inside the Covenanters Prison, he must have disappeared into thin air because there's no way out in the far right of the area, I even had a strange feeling while passing, something didn't feel right. I didn't call out, as he appeared quite suddenly on the right-side walking briskly away from us and took a right turn at the end. I was stunned because my mother didn't see anything. There were no birds singing and clouds had covered the sun. I felt strange. When he disappeared, the birds began singing again and the clouds disappeared. He was a tall man, with a black coat and a black top hat. It was in late August 2019. I don't know what to make of it, but I know what I saw.' Interestingly an image of the hat was then posted online revealing one which a quaker might have worn.

Our next account sent to me by musician and artist Mark Fernyhough, took place in 2019. In the company of his friend

Susan Sloan, they were enjoying a stroll in the Kirkyard. This is what he said: 'My friend Susan and I decided to take a closer look at the Mackenzie mausoleum after hearing much ghostly lore surrounding the tomb, it was indeed a location I was intrigued by. Despite its gothic exterior I had assumed it to be merely a tourism trap rather than an authentically supernatural site, however this perspective swiftly changed as we heard a bloodcurdlingly loud bang inside. Meanwhile Susan who was peering into the darkness of the tomb via the grills located on the towering doors witnessed something rapidly move across her line of vision. She described what she saw as a fuzzy white shape like a photo which had been partially developed.' He then went onto say that despite it being a beautiful day, the whole mood of the area changed and was, 'instantly transformed in an incredibly ominous environment.' He concluded by saying, 'we were quick to head out of the cemetery gates and back into the land of the living, where 17th century poltergeists are a less prominent blight on the landscape.'

During our conversation the subject of timeslips came up and although the following took place much further afield in his former home, Berlin, I felt inclined to use it as a good example. Residing in one of the older quarters, he described the apartments as being of an impressive scale. On one occasion, his upstairs neighbours leaving for a trip asked if he would keep an eye on their flat. Not adverse to a little house-sitting Mark agreed and was given a spare set of keys. One evening, while sitting in his flat he was greatly perturbed by the sound of thumping boots from his neighbour's property. Perplexed at the increasing racket, he debated whether to investigate but was nervous of doing the this. Questions raced through his mind. Who was up there? Would they be dangerous? Were they friends of the owners? And why were they singing in Russian? They certainly appeared to be drunk as the sound of their singing and carousing filled the air. The noise went on unabated for what seemed like hours and then abruptly stopped. A tentative look revealed, their flat pristine and silent as before and on seeing this, Mark left swiftly. On the owner's arrival some days later, the reluctant house sitter went to return the keys and in doing so broached the subject of what he had heard. The couple studied him intently, replying that they always knew the flat had a strange atmosphere at times. They went onto say that as Berlin fell to the allies, Russian troops had apparently been billeted in the then ruinous apartments, no doubt carousing celebrating and singing Russian songs ...

After reading of his exploits for years, I have concluded that the Mackenzie poltergeist, may just be the Elvis of the Scottish ghost world and is truly a case where its infamy has preceded itself, but what it/he is remains resolutely unclear. It continues to inspire a media frenzy and most investigations are still regarded as inconclusive. Is it a spirit or perhaps something more malignant? Certainly, its reputation and countess attacks suggest the latter. The attacks are random when it comes to the age and sex of the victims, and considering these disparities, the case is likely to remain unsolved. Some argue that it could be a mass hallucination, but this seems unlikely, and I suspect in fifty years we will be no nearer the truth. For those of nervous disposition it is perhaps best avoided for those braver, I heartily recommend a visit.

For our final account, I have included the following described to me by mesmerist and magician Mark Edward Wilson. Being from the U.S and having an interest in genealogy,

Mark set out to discover his past. Sometimes one can find surprising results and it came as quite a shock to discover that his oldest known ancestor was one Margaret Wilson, a supporter of the Covenant, executed in 1685. Her manner of passing was brutal even for the times, being held forcibly under the encroaching waves of the Solway Firth. Chained to a post, she was drowned at the age of eighteen, then laid to rest in Wigtown churchyard.

Mark told me, that the following bizarre set of events were set in motion when he accidentally discovered some of his late father's research. The paperwork which he described as literally falling out of a folder, had been sitting on a dusty shelf since 1989 and up till that point he knew nothing of Margaret. Attending a gathering of magicians/illusionists in Edinburgh circa 2001, he decided to take the file along for some light reading. Afterwards he paid a visit to Greyfriars. This is what he told me: 'I walked past a blackened building which looked to be a church or a large assembly structure. It wasn't just the wet streaks and cold stains that made it appear empty and dark. I resolutely felt a distinct vibration of utter misery emanating from it and something damp and dreadful came over me. This was especially present when I stood directly in front of an engraved bronze plaque with raised written markings and hundreds of names. Those names meant nothing, and I assumed they were buried inside.'

Leaving the cemetery, he then went to prepare for a planned dinner engagement. Over the course of the evening, he was introduced to a local and his son and during the conversation the subject of ghosts came up. He then mentioned his illustrious ancestor Margaret Wilson and of his family tree research. The locals seemed particularly drawn to this aspect of the conversation and knowing something of the subject proceeded to recount the tale of the Solway martyr as she was known. They intimated that the superstitious locals had thought of her something more than an overzealous eighteen-year-old, and that perhaps there was a darker side to the story. Mark then described what he had felt within the Greyfriars earlier that day, to which he noted both father and son, 'exchanged wide-eyed glances.' The next day prior to re-turning home, he felt a strange compulsion to visit the kirkyard again and in doing so searched for the plaque, find-ing the name Margaret Wilson.

It was not until fourteen years later that Mark returned to Edinburgh. Again, it was work related and as before visited the cemetery, this time with friends. Once inside he made a startling discovery as neither he nor his companions could find the plaque. Questioning why such an imposing historical monument would have been demolished he secured the help of the nearby beadle and enquired as to the location of the plaque. Had it been moved? And where was the building he had observed on his previous visit? The beadle appeared puz-zled and stated that he must be mistaken as neither of these things existed! The Covenanters he was told had been held in a nearby field, now at the top end of the cemetery, but he had no knowledge of Margaret Wilson nor the plaque. Mark wrote later, 'I wondered if it was false memory syndrome, a strange hallucination. It was as if Margaret Wilson and her history found me and exerted her influence, there can be no doubt about that. I know what I saw. I know what I felt.'

Intriguing to say the least but let us not despair as I will finish on a lighter note. I took a tour around November 2020, after the then Covid Lockdown had eased and as usual I ended up at Greyfriars cemetery. I remember it being a chilly and dark evening and that a few straggling leaves still clung to the nearby trees. At the starting point a couple who seemed very interested in the paranormal had joined the tour. I quickly got the impression they were a little overwrought and several times they asked me if we might see a ghost on the tour. This had not gone unnoticed by the rest of the participants, but I tried to be as gentle as possible suggesting it might be unlikely and so with that in mind we set off. Near the climax of the tour, we arrived at the churchyard and veered left along the path towards the Flodden wall. On arriving at a very dark and desolate Covenanter's prison, it became apparent that the couple were nowhere to be seen. Puzzled momentarily I then carried on as before describing the aforementioned break-ins. I then recounted the severed head story before moving on towards the small herb garden situated near the main gate, I had just begun my finishing speech when it was cut short by an ear-piercing shriek. The group nearly jumped a foot in the air and their nervous eyes darted like startled goldfish above their masks. The shriek which appeared to have come from the direction of the Flodden wall, was soon followed by the sound of thundering feet and from the darkness we witnessed the couple bolting towards us. The man, much taller led the charge and on arrival slipped in the mud before floundering into the herb garden. For a moment I wondered how the 'Friends of Greyfriars' might react to seeing the remains of their crop being trampled underfoot but had little time to dwell on the matter as the breathless woman now arrived. Obviously scared and hyperventilating, I forgave her impetuousness, when she suddenly clutched my arm. Barely able to speak she then began pointing towards the Flodden wall and croaked, 'there's a ghost standing by the wall, a ghost with an unnaturally white face.' The group looked nervous, and in a moment of bravado I suggested we go look. And that's when the great ghost hunt began, with near fifteen participants now creeping up the path in the pitch dark. Imagine Scooby-Doo and you will get the picture. After a few moments we arrived at our destination only to find 'the ghost,' was just a bloke having a fag. He looked a little taken aback, I must admit and perhaps thought we were ghosts? Afterwards, and to salvage the couple's dignity I suggested that it was an easy mistake to make, while those less forgiving chuckled merrily. I hope if reading this they can forgive me, but I include it as a salutary lesson in having a healthy dose of scepticism.

To conclude our brief visit to Greyfriars, perhaps my most frightening experience occurred some two years back. At the end of the tour and on a cold grim night I had made my tip speech and now waited expectantly to be showered in gold, like the Danae of old. The participants shuffled forward obligingly until it was the turn of two gentlemen. They were residents of Stockbridge no less, detectable by their plum-coloured corduroy breeks, and on finishing the tour furnished me with a 50p coin. Speechless at the sheer affront I mumbled my thanks. I thought afterwards, that to be insulted thus by someone poor one can cope with, but to be insulted by a 'toff!' is wholly abhorrent!`

Going Underground: The Vaults

B ack on the Royal Mile is our next destination, or there-abouts, as we pay a visit to one of Edinburgh's most popular tourist attractions, the South Bridge vaults. The vaults, now entered by both Blackfriars and Niddry street, were initially the nineteen arches of the newly constructed South Bridge. Measuring 1078ft in length by around 40ft high it was an astonishing feat of engineering, but on completion was regarded as a cursed bridge and so locals continued to take the circuitous route through the Cowgate to avoid it. Their reason for doing so or so it has been said, was because the first person to cross it, did so in their coffin. The story goes that the dearly departed, a respected judge's wife, was promised the task of cutting the ribbon as it were and was to be the first to cross the newly opened bridge. The grim reaper had other plans however and she passed away shy of the bridges opening. Despite this unfortunate turn of events, the powers that be felt obligated to keep their promise and so on the day, she rode across in her funeral coach. At least the speech would have been short. Soon after completion, the awe-inspiring structure vanished on the construction of the tenements we see today, creating hidden chambers which functioned as both storage and business premises. They soon became unusable due to water ingress, the persistent rain creating very damp unpleasant surroundings. The legitimate businesses which vacated were soon replaced by those less fussy, the underbelly, though not the ubiquitous event's organisers but rather the underbelly of society. Today we can only guess at the quality of life for those who called it home, but the few descriptions that remain paint a shocking picture of deprivation, drunkenness and prostitution. The overcrowding would have been abominable. This was an environment where people could disappear permanently and leave no trace. It took many years to oust the rabble and when they did the cellars and connecting doors were abandoned and forgotten, the vaults now filled with rubble. Largely forgotten until being re-discovered by ex-Scottish International Rugby player Norrie Rowan in the 1980's, this story has been well documented, so for now let's focus on some eyewitness accounts.

Now home to three tour companies, they are ideal location for ghost tours, which of course they play up to, some employing actors to deliver the ghostly goods. There's also the bonus of potentially running into some of the city's most infamous ghosts including 'the Watcher,' 'Mr. Boots' (potentially one and the same) the 'lady in blue' and even George Mackenzie. Tales abound, and though certain tours are at times gimmicky, there is no denying the inherent creepiness of the vaults. The tunnels both claustrophobic and chilly, can be disorienting and so are not to everyone's taste but for those hoping to catch a glimpse of the otherworldly they can rest assured, the ghostly residents are still very much front and centre.

Take for example this account from Helen McFarlane who described to me her visit to the vaults in May 2011. Helen, who had been on an Auld Reekie ghost tour witnessed a series of inexplicable events which made it an unforgettable experience. On entering they were led into a tiny room set out like a torture museum. The floor which was wooden appeared to be very creaky and so any movement was easily detectable. This is what she said. 'There were four people in front of me and a couple of girls behind as we stood in the space. There would have been about a 2m distance between everyone. I suddenly felt a playful punch on the back of my shoulder and glanced back to see if anyone in the group had moved. They were all standing in the exact same spot, and I am sure I would have heard the floor creak had they moved.'

Further on while the group were treated to a grisly tale involving the great fire of Edinburgh, Helen's nostrils were assailed by the smell of burning, so potent in fact, that she enquired if any staff members had set off a firecracker to achieve the intensity. The staff of course were quick to refute this, however the smell continued while they remained within the space. Soon after the phenomena continued as they now stood in two groups at opposing sides of a room. A sudden intense pushing on her lower back swiftly became painful due to its intensity. She said afterwards that it felt like someone had wanted her out of the room, though those nearest to her seemed unaware of what was happening.

Abi Franklins story, which is next, featured recently in an article in the Edinburgh Evening News. In it she described a photograph she took while touring the vaults of what appeared to be a figure. She recounts: 'We once visited the vaults on Southbridge. I stood at the door of a tiny, smelly, pitch-black room, supposedly haunted by a woman whose husband had been tortured and killed and the children taken away because they couldn't pay their illegal landlord. The first photo I took showed nothing but an empty room. Then I took another (the image clearly shows a hand with a lace type sleeve at the wrist floating in the darkness) and on seeing it my blood ran cold and I couldn't sleep all night. Since then, I have had the photo looked at by both a tour guide and a historian, but no one can explain it.' Having scrutinised the image, I have to say it looks very intriguing and is considered a great example of a potential ghost photograph.

Like Abi, Niki Hays experiences also featured in the Edinburgh Evening News. In her report she recounted the tale of an alleged spirit boy who supposedly haunts the area. She found out later he apparently likes to hold hands with female visitors. This is what she said. 'I went on this tour and the whole time my left hand was freezing, when I left, I said goodbye to the child and the temperature in my hand went back to normal.'

It would also appear that the spirits do not differentiate between tourists and employees. Take Stephanie for example, who had the pleasure of working in the vaults for around five years. She stated: 'I heard someone growl in my ear once, which is something that has been reported by people on tours. I have seen a pale faced lady with short dark curly hair who I convinced myself wasn't there due to a trick of the light, though a lady matching this description has been seen by others. A girl on a tour also once said they saw a woman standing behind me which forced me to look over my shoulder for weeks. Probably the scariest moment I had was when everyone reacted to someone running through the group, we all heard the footsteps running up to and through the group. They freaked out and someone felt it ran through them, I have never had a reaction like that before.'

Alarming as this might seem to most there are other entities or spirits who perhaps are not so gentle and are seen as lower entities. Take for example an area known as the Pagan Circle. Situated in a low vault and notorious among the ghost-hunting fraternity. It allegedly got its name from a Pagan group who claimed they had trapped a demonic entity within the circle. The circle today takes centre stage on some tours and one can sometimes be asked to volunteer to stand within it. As a guide, I have spoken to many hundreds of people over the years and have often enquired if they had visited the vaults. If they have, I then ask what happened at the pagan circle? From what I have been told a good proportion of visitors who step inside or stand near it are prone to nausea, have migraines, collapse or feel nothing. It's around a fifty/fifty split. I have had first-hand experience of this and once witnessed my wife become faint near that very spot so I know only too well how distressing this can be. The incident took place around fifteen years ago and I might add neither of us had any knowledge of the area. We had arrived in the city and deciding to do a tour we literally picked one out of the hat. It proved to be interesting, and after exploring a few of the larger vaults we eventually reached the infamous circle. I remember the light being subdued and as we stood at the back my wife began to feel dizzy and staggering had to sit down. It was not the nicest of experiences and at first, I thought she had fallen ill. She told me on her recovery that she felt a pressure upon her shoulders as if someone had squeezed them. Afterwards my wife was convinced that something out of the ordinary had happened and has unsurprisingly shown little inclination to return. Another example was cited by Tabitha Milne who visited the vaults some years ago with her then partner. Neither had any knowledge of the area and so there were no expectations before their visit. Her partner an ex-soldier and very pragmatic was standing in the vicinity of the circle, when like many before him he suddenly went 'as stiff as a plank' before falling to the ground. On recovering the bewildered visitor could not explain what happened having never fainted before, though later suggested it may have been the heat. Tabitha was keen to point out that whole area was freezing throughout the tour. She also told me that her ex-partner, having served on the frontline, was not the type of guy to be fanciful.

The area has been visited on numerous occasions and scientists suggest the reason for the phenomena may be because of the 'stone tape theory.' This theory made famous by Nigel Kneale's 1972 play of the same name, suggested that recordings from the past are retained within the fabric buildings and can replay in the right circumstances. It is, some argue an entirely plausible theory. The play has since gained a cult following and is disturbing in part though unfortunately the kind of television you don't see today. Since then, scientists and parapsychologists have suggested that the low-level frequencies stored within certain types of rock can cause disorientation and create hauntings. But perhaps this is too neat an explanation. Perhaps recordings from the past are responsible for some alleged ghost sightings, but what happens when said spirit interacts? The following account took place in the vaults and was relayed to me by a visitor who was in no doubt as to what she saw.

One evening I was conducting a ghost tour and we had just entered Lady Stairs close off the Lawnmarket. Although nowhere near the South Bridge an American lady in our group seemed quite keen on my stories concerning the Vaults. Being American, she was not the most reserved. She then piqued my interest by stating, that if she hadn't have gone on the vaults tour the previous night, she would have thought the content of my tour was, and I quote, 'a load of crap.' I asked her to elaborate, and the group fell silent in anticipation. As it transpired, she had until two days ago thought the whole ghost thing was rubbish, being very sceptical and dismissive of the subject. The group now hooked drew closer as she went on to describe her tour and what the guide had related. Part way through his discourse she then noticed a woman dressed in blue standing behind him, though remained unaware of her presence and continued talking. After a while she noticed that the woman, who she assumed to be a member of staff kept staring at her. She was completely solid and was described as having dark hair and a high-collared dress. After several minutes of this she began to feel uncomfortable and then angry, so stared back. She stated, 'I was so pissed off that I ended up in a staring contest.' Unable to hold the women's gaze however she blinked, and on looking back the woman had vanished. Her startled expression then drew the attention of the guide who after holding her back asked what she had seen. As she began to describe the woman he interjected, asking if she had been wearing a blue dress and at the affirmative his eyes glinted merrily. Half laughing, he assured her that it had not been a member of staff but rather a ghost, one, which according to her description had been seen on numerous occasions. Strangely all the witnesses have until now been woman, predominantly in the mid-twenties age range. Why,

I have no idea? I have often told this story on subsequent tours though on the whole people might assume I made it up, but I didn't and the look in the witnesses' eyes as she related her story, said it all.

We're Going on a Ghost Hunt

I n this chapter, we now look at the art of 'ghost hunting.' I'm not a particular fan of the term but nevertheless for the sake of simplicity I will stick with it. The investigators goal of course, is to ultimately prove the existence of ghosts, though up till now this has proved elusive. It is perhaps more to do with gravy than grave as someone once said, or words to that effect. The line which I have just paraphrased comes as I am sure you are aware, from a 'A Christmas Carol.' Recognised as being one of the earliest, if not the earliest Christmas ghost story, the inspiration for its title character lies closer to home than might be imagined, Canongate cemetery to be precise. Situated near the bottom end of the Royal Mile it is the last resting place of one, Ebenezer Lennox Scroggie, a former Lord Provost. Scroggie, born in nearby Kirkaldy, died in Edinburgh in 1836 and his occupation was a meal man or corn merchant and importer of wines and spirits. His headstone which has been described as 'misplaced,' was probably crushed to rubble in a reconfiguration of the cemetery earlier last century. This is a pity as I'm sure it would have been a great draw for fans of the writer. In one of his frequent visits to the area the myopic Charles Dickens apparently mis-read the meal man inscription, thinking it read mean man. Left pondering as to the character of Scroggie and why he had gained such a poor epitaph he wrote afterwards, "it must have shrivelled Scroggie's soul to carry such a terrible thing to eternity." With those thoughts firmly embedded in his mind he became the namesake of the vile Scrooge, despite Scroggie's well-documented good nature and jovial personality. What must he have thought?

Anyhow, whether you hope to prove the existence of spirit for religious purposes or debunk the notion of afterlife through scientific study, Edinburgh is the place to be. One of the few cities where one can study parapsychology, the world-famous Koestler Institute has been long established in the city. I contacted Professor Caroline Watt at the institute to find out a little more about their objectives and though I had assumed rather naively, that in the past they had set up home here due to the reputation of the city, I was soon put straight. Below is part of the transcript.

Question: 'Have you ever been contacted by a member of the public who has become anxious due to what could be termed anomalous phenomena?'

Answer: 'If contacted by a distressed member of the public we could ask them if they would like to speak to a colleague, a clinical psychologist with over forty years' experience. Often, we find that if people try to keep a diary or a photographic record, this makes the events decline and eventually cease. Some parapsychologists, Walter Von Lucadou for example, thinks that for theoretic reasons paranormal phenomena are by nature elusive and so will decline if placed under close observation. Research suggests that around 50% of those who contact parapsychologist units under distress may be suffering from a psychological or psychiatric condition.'

Question: 'Have you ever in your experience or that of a colleague, studied anyone you believe to have possessed heightened senses you could describe as, unusual?'

Answer: 'I have not personally, however I know of a couple of colleagues who believe they have witnessed individuals with exceptional abilities.'

Question: 'Do you know of anyone in the field of parapsychology who has strong religious beliefs, and do you think it's possible to hold both scientific and religious views?'

Answer: 'I don't know specifically regarding parapsychology. But there are scientists who hold both views and seem to manage.'

Question: 'Have you ever had a paranormal experience yourself?'

Answer: 'I have occasionally conducted controlled laboratory studies in Edinburgh where the results support the hypothesis of paranormal ability.'

Question: 'Edinburgh has a reputation as being rife with supernatural occurrences. Do you think because of this, the idea that paranormal occurrences are real is ingrained in people's psyche?'

Answer: 'This kind of Reputation is deliberately fostered in order to attract tourists and make money. I think most people take it with a pinch of salt. I think we are all susceptible to irrational thought, but if we are educated, we may be able to counterbalance with our understanding of processes that can contribute to the term, "what's not psychic but looks like it." This saying is credited to my mentor Professor Robert Morris.'

Around ten years ago, Edinburgh was home to 'Ghost fest.' As the name suggests, it was a festival devoted to all things ghostly, including vigils, tours and other spooky based shows. Though short lived it was an opportunity for like-minded people to explore the darker side of the city. If I remember correctly it ran for several weeks and the most sought-after events were the overnight vigils which sold out quickly. It was a tempting prospect and on one occasion, along with my like-minded pal Colin, we duly paid our £80 entry fee. The investigation was at the South Bridge vaults but on arrival my enthusiasm was somewhat dampened at the sheer volume of attendees. I could detect by their accents that they had travelled far and wide to attend and my fellow investigators included Liverpudlians, Yorkshiremen, 'Geordies', Londoners and a smattering of Scots. We were a motley group. The hosts, a professional 'ghost hunting' team quickly ran through the program for the evening which included both organised group activities, culminating with an opportunity to wander through the vaults. We were told a few tales to set the mood before one investigator stepped forward and opened a case. Inside sat an array of tech and after a brief explanation I duly received my temporary gift. Within seconds its purpose was lost to me and as suspected was akin to giving a chimp a clarinet, no disrespect to chimps. And so, for the next three hours we paced the vaults in the semi dark occasionally stopping to coyly ask if anyone was there. The silence was deafening. Somewhat aggrieved I began to surreptitiously listen to my fellow investigators, lurking within earshot in the hope of a vicarious thrill. They seemed oblivious to my presence, and I sourly noted each of their successes. One of them even threw a stone and claimed a ghost chucked it back. I'd had enough and sat sulking in the dark. As I sat there, I began to think about what I find scary and realised it was quite a lot. The list included heights, deep water, with or without sharks, flying and rap music. I could go on, but at the risk of sounding neurotic I will leave it at that. I also have a fear or at least feel uneasy about loud noises in darkened places and dislike the idea of loud music drowning out what I can't hear. I then realised it probably stems from when I was a kid. Being too young to get into pubs I was at that awkward age where you spend an inordinate amount time either sitting in bedrooms or wandering the streets aimlessly. One evening myself and my pal were as usual mooching around and, on that occasion, were on a street called Chattan Place. This was in my hometown of Aberdeen. While we were there my pal then suggested we go and explore the derelict builder's yard which sat further along. At first, I refused, but after some mild name calling in which my manliness came into question I agreed. We soon scaled the wall that surrounded the building, and after our feet struck the concrete of the weed strewn yard we crept slowly across. Ahead sat the darkened office complex, single storied and near ruinous. My pal having been there before, produced a candle from his jacket which he swiftly lit. Holding it aloft we crept along the main corridor casting grotesque shadows in our wake, and on reaching the end took a sharp right. Straight ahead lay our destination, a small windowless room. On entering he then placed the candle on a nearby desk. A light breeze coming from somewhere made the flame dance, every so often threatening to go out and terrible thoughts began to crowd my brain. What if were not alone? What if there was a murderer hiding in one of the darkened rooms? I began to think of the horror stories I had heard on the news, of kids disappearing, and on the verge of hysteria suggested we go. Incredulous at my suggestion, my friend then began to shout and scream clapping his hands to unnerve me, which he did. He was always a bit like that. Of course, I couldn't hear anything above the din which now echoed horribly in the enclosed space, and in my mind the corridor was alive with God knows what creeping towards me. I have always had a good imagination.

A sudden noise brought me back to reality and I was sitting with my back against the wall of the South Bridge Vaults. It was then I realised why I had an issue with investigations, what irked me was noise. Whether berating or challenging, the technical equipment peeping or people screaming, there was constant noise. And as dawn approached and time slowly crawled towards the finishing post the group began to gather their belongings. We smiled, wished each other well and hobbled off towards a well-earned rest. It was a cold morning if I remember, and it was obvious by the excited chatter that some of the participants had a more fruitful night.

I've been lucky to have had a few 'ghost hunts' under my belt and they've been a real eye opener, occasionally an eye closer. In my experience, a paranormal group usually consists of a mix of sceptics and believers. Perhaps they may also have in their ranks a medium or sensitive, to provide balance. I attended a nearby church some years ago and was hugely impressed by some of the evidence given and I personally know some individuals who have great mediumistic abilities. Sometimes though one is left puzzling and here is a good example. My place of work around seven years ago was a late medieval gaol, and of course was thought to be haunted. It was occasionally used as a location for overnight investigations. I used to enjoy these experiences and being paid for the privilege was a bonus. On one occasion there was a large crowd present, a mixture of team members and the paying public and during the night we tried several experiments. The 'guest' mediums were naturally, the most flamboyant in the room, the first making numerous inaccurate proclamations. Perhaps she was having an off night which happens, though her denial in the face of overwhelming evidence as to what purpose the gaol had been built for, proved the final straw. Exhausted, she then retreated to the ground floor, only to be replaced by another. He was a large fellow, certainly not medium and possessed a loud voice. We stood in awe at a safe distance, in respect for our ears as he described what he was feeling. He then indicated we should go to a certain room, where hung a collection of portraits of previous Lord Provosts. On entering and much to our surprise, he began to scream dramatically and berate the image of one poor fellow. Addressing the portrait, he shrieked 'bastard' at the top of his lungs as the stunned group looked on. Their expressions in the half- light bore a look of surprise, while the provost's expression thankfully remained composed. I began to wish the inaccurate medium would re-appear but there was no sign of her and the chap now sweating profusely moved in for the kill, insisting that provost had accosted numerous women while in office. To add further drama to the proceedings, he then began to claw at his head as if trying to empty his brain of those thoughts. It was a magnificent performance rounded off by a challenge to the dear departed to show himself. The former Provost sensibly declined and who could blame him, the sight of an eighteen stone Glaswegian sweating profusely being enough to alarm anyone. I hasten to add there was no evidence to substantiate his claims.

Despite this we should be eternally grateful to those who lead the way in the field of psychic research or ghost hunting, which includes such giants as, Wentworth-Day, J Thurston Hopkins, Eliot O' Donnell, Harry Price, Peter Underwood, Catherine Crowe, to name but a few. Anyone with a passing interest in the subject will be aware of their contributions, and their hair-raising encounters have provided many a sleepless night. So, on that note let's look at some of their contributions which have added to the mythos of Edinburgh's haunted heritage.

Catherine Crowe, one of the first woman to popularise the subject is recognised today for her seminal work, 'The Night Side of Nature.' A resident of Edinburgh for some years, she took full advantage of the city's predilection for all things paranormal by investigating several high-profile cases including the infamous Trinity poltergeist. Trinity at the time was around two miles from the city centre and in June 1835 home to Captain Molesworth, who lived in a rented property with his invalid daughter. His landlord literally within earshot lived next door as the substantial building had been reconfigured into two. As is the case in many accounts, all was well at the beginning, but before long unaccountable noises were heard. They assumed at first, they were being made by their landlord Mr. Webster, so took little heed. Thin walls have always been a problem in Edinburgh as I can testify, but these unaccountable sounds soon took the form of strange rapping's. At first Molesworth somewhat intrigued, began replying to the knocking which then responded to basic questions. Molesworth thought it peculiar though continued with his experimentation. Over time the raps increased with such ferocity that he approached the landlord. One can only imagine the conversation that day but suffice to say the landlord was indignant and protested his innocence. Molesworth, we assume, being in possession of a suspicious nature then took to drilling holes in the walls from which he could keep an eye and ear on proceedings. This did not go down well, further irritating the landlord. Soon afterwards the phenomena ramped up dramatically including beds being heaved upwards as if someone had hidden beneath. Molesworth, then in desperation, enlisted a group of friends and allies from nearby Leith Fort who formed what was described as a human cordon around the building. The purpose of this move remains unclear, though I suspect it gave local gossips value for money.

But there was worse to come as Molesworth now in mental disintegration turned his ire on his invalid daughter. We will never know how much of the story is true, or how much it has been exaggerated, but it is assumed he began to see her as the cause of the haunting. In a fit of delusion, he then resorted to tying her up within a bag, convinced that she was somehow responsible and according to reports she passed away soon after. A court case soon followed, and with it an associated media circus which gripped the Trinity area. Idling crowds now loitered in the vicinity hoping to glimpse something of the famed poltergeist. Meanwhile the landlord wanting his pound of flesh sought compensation for the criminal damage, the walls of his property wouldn't repair themselves. Molesworth's subsequent opinion of events and its outcome has never been recorded and so today, like with any aged tale, the truth remains questionable. Poltergeist activity is an accepted yet misunderstood phenomena and perhaps one of the most frightening. Regarded as being a directionless, violent entity, it has a propensity to attach itself to families and particularly younger girls, why remains uncertain. Other notable locations within Auld Reekie that have become synonymous with poltergeist activity include Hazeldean Terrace, Blacket Place,

Candlemaker Row, Victoria Street and Learmonth Gardens, some of which I will touch on later.

In a bizarre twist of fate, the author Catherine Crowe herself came under scrutiny some years later though not for the validity of her stories, but rather for the vicious rumours concerning her mental health. According to written allegations at the time, she was found wandering naked through the streets of Edinburgh having gone mad and subsequently placed in an asylum in Hanley. The story greatly exaggerated of course did Crowe a great disservice, but what is more surprising is that the flame of gossip was fanned by none other than the inventor of the Christmas ghost story, Charles Dickens. The author, already a successful writer had huge reservations about spiritualism and as such was prone to make caustic statements about those, he thought were supporters. As an advocate of mesmerism, a forerunner to hypnosis, he believed that the phenomena associated with the spiritualist movement could be easily replicated by stage magic. As a contributor to the Zoist, a magazine devoted to this 'new science' he was prone to hold court and being a boy's club of sorts, he was not above spreading a little gossip especially if it involved a woman. Crowe's name was therefore dragged through the mire in a series of defamatory letters and articles. One such letter read.

'Mrs. Crowe has gone stark mad, and stark naked on the spirit rapping imposition. She was found t'other day in the street, clothed only in her chastity.' This was closely followed by, 'There is a certain Mrs. Crowe usually resident in Edinburgh, she was a medium, an ass, and I don't know what else. The other day she was discovered walking down her own street in Edinburgh, not only stark mad, but stark naked too.'

Ouch! Why he latched onto her with such vitriol and not anyone else with similar beliefs is open to speculation, but I suspect misogyny played its part. The truth of the matter is less salacious however, and it is thought that Crowe, who after suffering from a short illness displayed signs of distress and mental instability which in turn caused great concern to her friends. In panic they took her to Handsell, a renowned hospital, thinking it the best course of action. There she was met by Dr Conolly who in a fit of rare judgement for the time declared it nothing more than a temporary aberration. After receiving a prescription, she was returned to full health where she continued with a successful writing career. What Dickens made of this or indeed what her opinion was of him afterwards will have to keep for another time.

Perhaps though the most prolific writer on the subject, was Elliot O Donell. Recognised as one of the most influential authors of supernatural fact and fiction, by the time of his death in 1965 he had amassed an impressive body of work most of which concerned the supernatural. Covering such diverse subjects as haunted trees, haunted castles, werewolves, Scottish Ghosts and London ghosts, he wrote with authority, proclaiming to have psychic abilities. Allegedly a descendant of Irish Royalty, he was a striking figure and was often invited to investigate haunted buildings. He moved in high circles and was well respected. In recent years however the authenticity of his 'true ghost stories,' have come into question, not only due to the sheer volume of stories he appeared to be personally involved with but because of their terrifying content. So horrific were they, that the great M R James himself, no stranger to the macabre wrote, "I sincerely hoped the ghosts described by O' Donnell were fictional, since life might otherwise become an extremely hazardous business." Either way the quality of his writing is admirable. He also ascribed to no societies preferring to operate in lone wolf mode, though cynics have argued it gave him carte blanche on reporting his findings. His stories which are at times beyond hair-raising contain scenarios his modern counterparts would no doubt give their eye-teeth for. This ambiguity has led to many questioning the authenticity of the stories, however there were apparently good reasons for his reticence. It appeared that some years previously he had confided in someone who let the cat out of the bag so to speak. The witnesses who wished to remain anonymous were then understandably vexed to find their name being bandied around in certain circles. Afterwards, with the threat of a lawsuit, a harsh lesson was learned. It was an age where propriety was to the fore and admitting to residing in a haunted house could at the very least reduce your standing in the community. O' Donnell would never make the same mistake again. Perhaps, you may think, this all sounds a little too convenient but bear in mind the case of Mr. Molesworth. I can understand his reticence as having interviewed hundreds of people over the course of the last fifteen years, there were still a surprising amount of those who wished to remain anonymous. Whether this is through fear of ridicule or not is open to question, but personally I can't see the logic. I would be quite happy to stay in a haunted house, provided the ghosts possessed good manners and in doing so would be equally delighted to tell the world! But people are strange and the older I have become the more I realise this. To me hiding your ghost stories seems a pity and if they are the only skeletons in your closet then you should be grateful. I have on more than one occasion been told amazing accounts, only then to have been asked not to publish them which was hugely frustrating. These have included accounts of two exorcisms, a haunted flat situated above a pub and a private home in which the stories are quite astonishing. They were well corroborated, the evidence overwhelming and still to this day I have been sworn to secrecy. I was also told of an incident which would involve a court case and 'financial ruin' for the witness if ever made public, which is a pity.

On this very subject, O' Donnell wrote, 'with this in view I cannot be surprised that the possessors of family ghosts and haunted households, show the greatest reluctance to be approached on the subject, save by those they feel assured will treat it with the utmost delicacy.' He went on to say, pre-empting another of his famous tales, 'The Sallow-Face Woman of Forrest Road.' 'Occasionally I have been taken in as to give permission for the writer to call on me, and almost always I have bitterly repented. The wily one-no matter how wily- cannot conceal the cloven hoof for long, and he has either tried to thrust himself into the bosom of my family, or has written to my neighbours declaring himself to be my dearest friend; and when in desperation, I have shown him the cold shoulder, he has attacked me virulently in some rag of a local paper, the proprietor, editor or office-boy of which happens to be of his own clique. I have even known an instance where this type of person through trickery, gained access to some notoriously haunted house, and from its owners, the family he has long had eyes on, from a motive anything but psychic-has ferreted out the secret and private history of the haunting.' He then went onto say that the stories have then been published in a most sensational manner! One might argue there's a certain irony in that statement, however the authors respect for the families who sought help seemed foremost and for that he must be applauded.

We will of course never know how accurate his stories are, but as a child, I had many sleepless nights because of him. I can recall quite clearly, lying with the covers firmly wrapped over my head in the aftermath of one of his tales. Even an adult I still find them so evocative, and their antiquarian creepiness makes me desperately want them to be true. In his book 'Scottish Ghosts,' he details accounts from across the nation stopping of at various points and of course duly arrives in Edinburgh. The stories from Auld Reekie are particularly shuddersome and after reading of Pringles Mansion and the bounding ghost of Buckingham Terrace, I wanted to see the locations for myself. Today, ironically, I live around the corner from the latter and often find myself idly wondering which building the story took place in.

Like Molesworth, the Gordons who rented the property were also threatened with libel for daring to suggest the house was haunted! The street today, Buckingham Terrace, has changed little since the time of the haunting. According to the account, the family were plagued by the sound of loud bounding footsteps on the communal stairs. After a time, they questioned the porter who appeared perplexed, perhaps it had been someone next door he suggested? The noises continued sporadically over the next while, sometimes lasting up to half an hour, but they remained no nearer to solving the mystery. The story then described how Diana the eldest daughter, witnessed a 'something.' Described as being indistinct and blurred it sprang out of a nearby room with a bound, went past her onto the landing, before ascending the stairs to the attic. Diana then summoning her last reserves of courage followed. Two floors above lay the attic separated from her home by the vacant flat below and on entering she again witnessed the entity. It now stood next to an antique eight-day clock which it appeared to be winding. With her nerves now at breaking point she sprang from the room and dashed to the safety of the ground floor where she and her siblings spent a sleepless night. As in all good ghost stories the denouement to the tale soon followed on the reappearance of the apish figure. Waking one night from a restless slumber, she was shocked to find a familiar figure slowly opening her bedroom door. In the half-light she could make out the extraordinary sight. It was dressed much like a sailor with pea jacket and large boots, while under one arm he held a bundle of red and white rags, and in the other a 'small bladder of lard.' The figure then turned and once again bounded upwards. According to the account, Mrs. Gordon left the next day despite the protestations of her irate landlord. Once safely vacated, it came to light that some years prior, a retired Sea Captain had rented the apartment. One of his eccentricities was that he always wore his seafaring boots, a reefer jacket and blue jumper. He was also known to drink and suffered from delirium tremens, and it was in one such state that he threatened the tenants above, a mother and baby. Soon after, while in an all-consuming rage he decapitated the infant because it would not stop crying then stuffing both the body and head within the clock. When apprehended he spent his remaining days within an asylum. A grim tale indeed though even Mr. O' Donnell ends by suggesting perhaps its authenticity should be questioned. It goes without saying that there is no hard evidence to back the tale up. Still, I often stand and ruminate on the spot and think what if?

But now we must move, and in doing so, take a brief nod to another prolific investigator and former president of 'The Ghost Club,' Peter Underwood. The club, still going strong is the oldest of its kind in the world and numbered among its members is a veritable who's who of investigators and authors. Underwood enjoyed a long and illustrious career, compiling many books on the subject which included the seminal, 'Gazetteer of Scottish Ghosts.' More prosaic in his description of alleged hauntings his stories are perhaps easier to believe, and many modern ghost hunters have no doubt avidly perused the pages of said tome. Described as a professional ghost hunter he set the standard for all that was to follow, and all in a time when the subject was looked on less favourably. This following story has been touched upon in several books including those of Underwood and is worth a revisit. This what is said to have happened.

The origins of the story lie in Sandwood bay near Cape Wrath and though geographically far from Auld Reekie, they share a connection. The area both wild and remote and consists of several lonely beaches sprinkled with the odd cottage and occasional hamlet. The aptly named Cape Wrath has been responsible for the loss of many ships, and subsequently there are several documented cases involving the sighting of ghostly sailors. Interesting as these stories are we shall not explore them further but suffice to say the bearded figures of old salts have been witnessed by many. In one instance a local man even described a weather-beaten face peering into his cottage and on investigation found nothing, while another woke to find something dark and ominous pressing down on him. I must admit this is how I felt in the run up to Brexit, but I digress. In his story, Underwood then went on to state that he had been contacted by a woman, a householder in both London and Edinburgh and one can only assume richer than Croesus. She had it transpired, been gifted with a small piece of wood taken from the staircase of a ruined cottage situated in Sandwood bay. On receipt of the gift, strange poltergeist activity then began to manifest in both her homes. This including loud footsteps at night, flying plates, (I wonder if they were saucers) and a gamut of the usual phenomena. In Edinburgh however the phenomena appeared more prevalent resulting in an incident in which she detected the smell of both tobacco and alcohol. On turning she witnessed a tall, bearded sailor, who after staring at her for some moments vanished promptly. After the piece of wood was put under lock and key the phenomena abated. Afterwards she could not be persuaded to visit the area, despite the intriguing connection. Strangely some years earlier another incident had occurred on the same beach. According to this report, a father and son were collecting kindling along the shore after leading their pony onto Sandwood Bay. After some time, the animal displayed signs of unusual nervousness before the figure of a man appeared. He demanded that; 'they take their hands off what doesn't belong to them and leave his property.' They complied rather hurriedly. Later he was described as a large, bearded sailor.

Before we move on to look at another 'haunted' artefact let's take a moment to remember another investigator who rightly sits among those previously mention, the great Sir Arthur Conan Doyle. Recognised for the creation of the world's greatest detective Sherlock Holmes, he was also a prolific author of adventure stories and supernatural fiction much connected to his spiritual beliefs. Having lost a son during The Great War, he like countless others turned to the spiritualism, embracing if fully though perhaps in some instances too readily. He wrote extensively on the subject and his book, 'The New Religion' along with Oliver Lodges, 'Raymond, Life and Death,' are regarded as compulsory reading. He is still a highly regarded figure in both a literary and spiritual sense which I suspect will never diminish and today remains a fascinating and inspirational character. His childhood home at Picardy Place, near Leith Walk is unfortunately now gone, however today we can console ourselves in the nearby pub which bears his name. In 2001, the Sir Arthur Conan Doyle Spiritualist Centre opened in Palmerston Place, its aim being to promote physical, mental and spiritual wellbeing. It is a broad church so to speak and is open and welcoming to all, irrelevant of faith and belief. They also have within its walls a psychic investigation unit (PIU) who like our friends, the parapsychologists are sometimes called upon to offer succour to those who believe their homes to be haunted. Much like the university they also promote the use of reflective diaries, recording dates, incidents and the wellbeing of the caller before making any judgment. Perhaps science and religion have some common ground after all? I have visited on several occasions and on entering one is struck by its unique atmosphere which suits the place well. It is also according to some, haunted, which I would expect given it's a spiritual haven. I concede that perhaps the word 'haunted,' is not the correct terminology a spiritualist might use, however for the purpose of this book it will do. It is doubtful that the spirit of the great man himself is permanently there as you can imagine, however a figure bearing an uncanny resemblance has been seen on occasion. It is also said he has come through during seances or platform work, no doubt happy to see his work continuing. Perhaps his ethos is best summed up by the following words: 'The most dangerous condition for a man or a nation is when his intellectual side is more developed than his spiritual. Is that not exactly the condition of the world today.'

Having already touched upon the dangers of proclaiming a house to be haunted I wanted to offer up one last example.

The following, though stretching credulity, happened, with the ensuing trial taking place in the Police Court of 1815. The following description of proceedings, republished in The Edinburgh Despatch of April 1933, if nothing else provides some amusement. The defendant, a 'gentleman's servant,' was accused of spreading malicious tales concerning the haunting of his master's house the New Towns Jamaica Street. News spread rapidly and because of this no one wished to take up tenancy. The owner seeking recompense through the courts strangely did not sack the offender, who on the day of the trial elected to defend himself against the 'heinous offence.' During proceedings he went on to describe his encounters with the spirit which he had seen twice. He then described it as being copper coloured and wearing a red nightcap. He then went on to say he had even conversed with it but being pressed upon to divulge the nature of the conversation, he refused to elaborate, stating he had, 'promised to keep it a secret.' I would have loved to have been there that day. The judge remained stony faced throughout and bound him over to keep the peace for twelve months. On leaving there were further surprises when the defendant asked if, with his honour's permission, 'might he be permitted to talk to the ghost again, since he had promised he would, and he had specifically been invited to partake in hospitality.' Unfortunately, the outcome of the conversation been noted. Did the hospitality involve spirits I wonder? For our next stop we now venture further afield to leafy Comely Bank, where things take a darker turn.

A Mummy's Curse?

As I sit writing this, I am aware that 500 yards along the road sits one of Edinburgh's most notorious, haunted homes, 15 Learmonth Gardens. Previously a home to Lord and Lady Seaton it was the scene of one of the most well documented cases in the annals of Edinburgh's ghostly cannon and eyewitness accounts continue to this day. The house, innocuous as its neighbours, is a three floored Sandstone building and so it is hard to imagine the reputation it once held, however, to begin the account let's look at its former owner. Sir Alexander Hay, 1st Baronet Seton to be precise was born in 1904 and by his passing in 1963 he had believed for a good proportion of his adult life, to have been placed under a curse. It all began in 1936 when Egyptology was at the height of fashion. Historians, archaeologists and scientists fascinated by a culture advanced for time, were actively plundering tombs and stealing artefacts to fill museums in the west. Who knows how many rare pieces were lost, sold by unscrupulous locals to like-minded tourists? For those in high society, a world of discovery lay within their means and as part of their own Egyptian odyssey, Seton and his wife Zeyla visited a temple at Luxor. Zeyla who was a social climber and go-getter, was delighted at the prospect. His memoirs which describe the incident also make no attempt to disguise the state of their marriage which at best could be described as fraught, and it was to be further tested on their return to Edinburgh.

Before this though, Seton described himself as being 'in a mood of complete satisfaction, caused by good eating, excellent brandy and the cool of the evening, but most importantly of all by the receipt of a very welcome cheque from a Glasgow editor, to whom I had sent a description of my journey.' With Luxor ticked off their itinerary they then returned to Cairo and in doing so were approached by one of their associates Abdul. He was a local man who intimated his brother could arrange for them to see a newly discovered tomb near the Great Pyramid. Lord Seton by his own account felt a little unsure of the offer but was browbeaten into going by his wife. In his biography, 'Transgressions of a Baronet,' he later explained. 'I had a feeling in my bones that something was going to happen over this, and it was only with the greatest difficulty that Zeyla cajoled me into going with her. I wish earnestly to God that we had not gone.'

Visiting the tomb, they described the burial as being 'Premummy,' and the corpse lying exposed and badly deteriorated was that of a high-class female though not royalty. The tomb cavernous and dank by all accounts, sounded suitably awe inspiring by his description and they spent some time examining the interior. Afterwards his wife who appeared particularly fascinated by the tomb, slipped back inside for one last look while he enjoyed a smoke outside. A visit to the pyramid souvenir shop was then proposed but to her husband's surprise Zeyla refused indicating she would prefer to return to their hotel. He obliged and it was only afterwards finding the reason why, she had already acquired her own souvenir.

This little memento of their visit turned out to be something quite unique. A vertebra belonging to the interred corpse. Seton by all accounts was aghast, but his wife strong -willed and fiery refused to take it back and insisted on keeping it. After all what harm could it do? Back in Edinburgh the bone was then placed inside an old clock case in their home and for some time it became the talking point of many a conversation. Seton not overly enamoured with the item, which he described as looking like a digestive biscuit, grudgingly housed it in his study. Soon after he regretted his wife's impulsive actions.

Soon after, the first incident of note occurred when departing guests were nearly struck by a large piece of chimney masonry falling from the parapet. Thankfully no one was injured, and the blame was placed firmly on the state of the building. A few nights later things took a turn for the worst when the first of a series of chilling encounters took place. In this instance their nanny came running up the stairs, blurting out that she had heard someone creeping about in the drawing room. With some trepidation a search was undertaken but nothing found. A few nights later more noises were heard followed by a series of loud crashes. The Baronet however remained in bed despite the disturbance, which I suspect would have been the best place to be. It wasn't till the morning when Zeyla entered the drawing room that the truth of the matter was revealed and calling quickly, she summoned her husband who was soundly chastised, being blamed for the upended table in the corner. Seton of course, I am sure, protested his innocence though I suspect she didn't believe him. Again, a period of calm followed until a few weeks afterwards when the sound of someone on the stair in the middle of the night, prompted Zeyla to investigate. Suspecting it was their nanny, she was no doubt perturbed to find the stair devoid of life. To add to her growing consternation, on the following night similar noises were heard once more.

In an interview with the Scottish Daily Express soon after, Seton elaborated further. The interview co-incidentally was held from his sick bed, this bout of poor health the result of the bone, or so he believed. This is what he said. 'I can't explain these things. I wish I could for my own piece of mind. I laughed at the idea at first but now I frankly confess I am a little scared of the thing. I would willingly give the bone to anyone who would promise to treat it with respect. I will not have it destroyed and I don't think it should be regarded as a joke and made a sort of party game.' The interviewer then asked whether there were any incidents of note he would like to elaborate on and he willingly obliged.

'We had a nine-year-old boy stay here once. In the middle of the night, we heard him screaming and found him cowering under his bed clothes. He said he had been to the bathroom and on the way had seen a figure in what he described as a big dressing gown going into the drawing toom. I went there and switched on the light and found no one.' It was a terrifying experience for all involved and one can imagine the palpable fear that must have descended upon the house as bedtime drew nearer. Soon after a female friend of the couple was invited to stay over and in the middle of the night was awoken by the sound of someone moving around. Thinking it was her hostess she arose and went to speak to her only to see a figure disappear into the drawing room. She plainly saw the figure standing at the table on which the bone rested and on flicking on the light found the room to be empty. This no doubt led to another sleepless night. It transpired during the interview that neither the boy nor the woman had been told about the bone in advance of their visit.

Seton continued, 'I asked (their friend) if it was a man or woman but she could not see its face though she described it as small. Soon after I took the bone to a surgeon I knew, who after examining it said it belonged to someone small in stature.'

A short while later, Setons nephew Alasdair Black came to stay who surprised his uncle at breakfast by calmly announcing, 'he had seen a funny dressed person going upstairs.' Seton alarmed at this revelation no doubt pressed for further details and wrote afterwards, 'he assured me that he had gone to the lower lavatory the night before and had seen this person. He didn't seem to be the slightest bit scared of it.' As you can imagine a slow insidious fear began to grip the household. The noises were now occurring frequently and the Baronet in desperation locked the drawing room, keeping the key upon his person. He then held a vigil in the hope of unravelling the mystery, but to no avail. On the second night however, Zeyla's cries brought him running, and they observed the sound of someone in the drawing room. Summoning the courage to open the door they found the room in disorder with chairs upset, books flung in all directions, 'and there in the middle of the chaos was that damn bone.' In the aftermath of this event no one could could deny what was taking place and the Baronet in desperation allowed his wife to contact a local soothsayer. The subsequent visit apparently changed nothing other than costing a pound.

Sometime later the bone was then given to a reporter and because nothing occurred while it was in his possession it was duly returned. The resultant article which the reporter then published did little to save the blushes of the Baronet who was regarded in certain quarters as a joke. Enticed by the lure of money he stated afterwards, 'I only wish I had a good agent; I could have made a fortune from it.' Having learned nothing, he then handed the relic over to another reporter this time from the Scottish Daily Mail. It was soon returned when the man fell seriously ill. A short while later news of the first reporter being seriously hurt in a car crash reached their ears. The events were now beyond co-incidence.

The phenomena now became more violent, resulting in frequent terrific crashes being heard throughout the night. On one such occasion the bone was found shattered. At his wits end and with the family under great duress he wrote secretly to an acknowledged expert, Dr Carter of Tutankhamun fame who later confirmed his fears. He assured Seton it was unlikely to stop unless the bone was returned. Backed into a corner and with no reprieve in sight he then contacted his uncle asking for help. His uncle, a Benedictine monk at Fort Augustus Abbey then performed a blessing, before burning the bone to ashes. His wife was furious on hearing the news, having been absent during his visit. After the bone was destroyed his family continued to suffer prolonged periods of illness, whether due to the vicissitudes of life we will never know. One thing for certain is that many of those associated with the family did end up having very bad luck, including tragic deaths, illness and divorce. The Baronet's final words on the matter summed it up nicely, 'I still think it was one of the most horrible experiences that I have been through, happening in the daytime and night.'

The experiences he recounted in 'Transgressions of a Baronet,' are fascinating and the reader, me included, will at times question his motivations. They obviously enjoyed luxury and being titled one would expect this. Keeping up appearances with their peers takes money and so on publishing a book of one's travels would be appealing to some. In the 1930s, travel and adventure for the lower classes was unheard of, so vicariously living off other people's experiences was perhaps better than having no experience all. And of course, let's not forget that the baronet was quite happy to recount his experiences at first only regretting it when he suffered some humiliation. He was certainly unimpressed by many of the articles which followed. Perhaps the lack of renumeration was the cause? We can only guess at his motivations, though he was astute enough to publish the full account in all its glory. I remember, like many others, reading this tale but little did I suspect that one day I would be living a mere stone's throw away. This quirk of fate has given me many opportunities to observe the building on passing and I often wonder if the phenomena has continued. Occasionally I have noticed some of the present occupants and have thought long and hard whether I should approach them and ask. Good manners of course have stopped me thus far. Imagine if you were the unwitting occupier of a house with such a reputation, yet you were unaware of its history? As the old saying goes ignorance is bliss. But the question remains, is it still haunted? The answer I am glad to say, is quite possibly, at least according to some recent reports. A ghost story or at least a curse story of this calibre deserves a long shelf life, and I was pleased to see the tale resurfacing recently in 'North Edinburgh Nightmares', a website (and book) produced by author and investigator John S. Tantalon. He has in recent years put together some very interesting online investigations and the accounts are presented in a very plausible manner. His coverage of the curse story is no exception, and it came with the bonus of a contemporary report. A contribution from the keeper of Egyptology at the National Museum also added a little gravitas to the proceedings, backing up facts which some may have found questionable. It was quite thought-provoking. Better still interviewer J E Ross recounted the tale in situ and at the time met with a current witness, named Mike. The witness, a Reiki practitioner, coincidentally visited the house in 2004. He knew nothing of its sinister reputation and had gone there on a work-related visit. During the Reiki session, the client in some discomfort, rose to get a glass of water and left Mike alone in the room. On turning he then described seeing a tall figure swathed in a shroud or veil of some kind standing in the corner of the room. When asked, if he could tell whether it was male or female, he was unsure but said it remained motionless throughout. Averting his eyes momentarily he turned away, but on looking back the figure remained still. Despite wanting to call out he remained paralysed until the form eventually vanished. He went on to state that at no point did it attempt to move or approach him, which must have been something of a relief. What struck me most during the interview was the expression in the witnesses' eyes, which said it all, he had been badly scared. It was without doubt a life changing experience and he never returned to the property. The client intimated afterwards that strange things had happened before and so in the spirit of decency, future appointments took place on neutral ground. As a footnote the interviewer then mentioned the outcome of a brief conversation with another current resident. They wished to remain anonymous but stated; 'daft things happen in this place all the time.' And so, in conclusion that is why I try to avoid walking past at night. Perhaps I'm too nervous?

Speaking of bones, I came across a similar story recently which involved a 'curse 'that predates the above by some years. Taking place in Edinburgh around 1920 the story appeared in the aptly named James Bones, 'Edinburgh revisited,' who was author of the better known 'Edinburgh perambulator.' In it he relates a tale concerning another cursed artefact, 'The Egyptian Necklace,' In the story the author describes how an articulated green beaded necklace once sent as a gift caused much disruption to the unwitting recipient. The artefact, thought to be around 30000 years old and found near Heliopolis, arrived after some months before the beginning of the Great War. The item was then described as 'forgotten about,' until 1920 when it was rediscovered in a drawer. Neither the lady in question nor her location was mentioned but in the account the recipient allegedly threw the necklace into the bin along with some torn letters. Why she took this course of action was never made clear, however we can draw our own conclusions. Later that night at around ten thirty while preparing for bed she felt another's hand place upon hers as it rested on the back of a chair. Soon afterwards she then became aware of a 'continuous rustling' coming from the basket. Suspecting the culprit to be a mouse, she cautiously inspected the contents but found nothing. She did however have a change of heart and retrieving the necklace put it aside for safe keeping. Not long after, her brother, described as a well-known Edinburgh doctor arrived and was told of the occurrence. Being a practical sort, he then volunteered to have it next to him on his pillow while he slept. According to his report for several nights afterwards he neither saw nor heard anything until some days later he was awoken by a light thud on his pillow, 'as if a hand had made a vigorous grab for it.' There then followed a series of tapping noises which travelled across the ceiling. Despite this, he insisted on keeping the necklace with him. On the second night he woke with a start to find the bed shaking violently from side to side before it stopped abruptly. Again, he described the feeling of being touched by a phantom hand which left him with a strange sensation of pins and needles, running from head to chest. Some days later he was alerted to the sound of sobbing coming from near the window, which according to his testimony lasted from 30-60 seconds. Afterwards the perplexed owner then decided to pass the necklace between a group of acquaintances to ascertain if the phenomena would be repeated. As expected, some did whilst others experienced nothing. One of the recipients, who shared a bedroom with her 11-year-old daughter described placing the necklace on a nearby chair, she was awoken sometime later by a series of sharp tapping, which was described as travelling up the walls and across the ceiling. On another occasion, she described 'flashes of light, flashing through her room, like wildfire.' The original owner hearing of these various reports erred on the side of caution and on the necklaces return had it disposed of in Loch Leven. We can only assume if the story is true, the necklace lies there to this day.

Ale and Farewell: Haunted Pubs

They say Edinburgh pubs are full of spirits and there's certainly some truth to this, and Auld Reekie boasts more than its share of both varieties. For me, there is something comforting about an old pub and the thought of generations imbibing together in dark smoke-filled rooms, while a fire crackles in the grate is very appealing. Of course, the traditional pub is somewhat scarcer since the introduction of the wine /sports bar, or indeed the gastro pub. Though nothing ever remains the same, I am blessed to have had many pleasant hours in such places and am grateful that Edinburgh still boasts an inordinate number of these characterful bars. In my opinion though a good pub is not only judged on its bill of fare but also its potential for spookiness, and a pub, like a theatre without a ghost, is a shameful thing indeed. I love haunted hostelries especially ones with a touch more mine ghost, than mine host. To this end, the following accounts have been taken from some of the capitals best known watering holes and in doing so I hope I have been able to add to an already impressive roster.

Our first stop is in Edinburgh's famed Grassmarket, greedily containing at least six haunted venues. The area, recognised as one of the city's most ancient thoroughfares has had a long and particularly dark history, playing host to executions, riots and murders. It was so impoverished that the citizens of the Royal Mile turned up their collective noses at its denizens describing them as the 'worms of the earth.' This was in part due to the muddy hollow in which they eked out their existence. Today the area thrives on tourism, and the hen and stag parties which frequent its hostelries add to the colour. We start our Journey at the White Hart Inn, winner of the 2005, Most Haunted Pub in Edinburgh Award. It is instantly recognisable because of its ornate frontage, featuring a splendid wooden portico which entices the thirsty traveller. Famous imbibers have included, poets Robert Burns, William Wordsworth, and the less genteel Burke and Hare. Suspected of enticing numerous unfortunates back to their home in nearby Tanners close for the mother of all night caps, they are regarded as two of the earliest recorded serial killers. The pubs today are mere shadows of their former selves, thankfully, and so we can only imagine the filth and the squalor of the time.

Thought to be home to a few lingering spirits there is one lady who occasionally has been seen within the premises, thought to have been a victim of the nefarious pair. How this conclusion has been reached is open to question, however in the world of ghosts an occasional leap of faith is perhaps needed. Unlike some of the more reticent spirits, she kindly appeared in a photograph some years ago. Taken by a young girl having lunch, the image has divided opinions and shows what appears to be a semi-translucent figure of a woman dressed in red. Ambiguous and perhaps a little blurry the photograph is nevertheless unusual as it shows what appears to be a well-defined hand. Some have argued that it's down to camera shake though the rest of the clientele appear in focus. It is an intriguing image, made more so, by the persistent rumours that a woman with a penchant for wearing red ended up on the anatomy slab of Dr Knox.

Other reports have included sightings of a phantom pair of legs, minus the top half of course, which is not as unusual as one might think, as I have personal knowledge of three such cases. These have included a pair of legs seen walking across a stage within a theatre, the figure of half a sailor seen sticking out from a windowless wall, and the top half of an elderly lady seen gliding across a floor. This could potentially be terrifying or absurd depending on your point view. It is believed that in each instance the ghost is reacting to a floor level or architectural feature from their time despite subsequent structural changes. Other phenomena have included sightings of shadow figures, a staple of any haunting, who vanish when followed and beer kegs being turned off. Ridiculous as it seems this is possibly the most common activity associated with pub ghosts and I guarantee that every hostelry featured will have had the same issue. I have come to suspect that spirits must have a sense of humour, if nothing else and probably have a good old chuckle at the expense of bar staff. I have spoken to many publicans over the years, and I've concluded that, the ghost itself isn't an issue but rather what it does to the kegs. Perhaps they are bored? Maybe there isn't that much to do in the afterlife? The question remains open.

Edinburgh loves its pubs, it must be said, every street and corner is home to a welcoming ale house or wine bar. Haunted pubs are of course particularly sought, and in a city that has so many, they jockey for position as Edinburgh's most haunted. Who has that honour is open to debate, as everyone has their favourite. The Grassmarket of course, having an abundance, has many to choose from including the charmingly named, 'The Last Drop.' Easily recognised by the twin nooses in the window, it's another example of the city's literal gallows humour, ironically the exact location of executions, being mere yards away. The ghosts, as of course they have ghosts, appear to be like those described in many nearby buildings and we can only wonder if they are one and the same. Next on our list is Maggie Dickson's which potentially falls into that bracket; however, it has got a unique history in its namesake.

Named after a poor unfortunate wretch who survived the hangman, her story is as much a part of Edinburgh's lore as that of notorious thief Deacon Brodie or Greyfriars Bobby. Accused of infanticide, a crime she most likely didn't commit and for concealing her pregnancy she was hung for her crimes. The distraught family were surprised during her wake however, when they heard movement from within the coffin and on opening the lid were astonished to find Maggie very much alive albeit with a twisted neck. Taken back to face justice, she was then granted her freedom having been already pronounced dead. Thereafter locals gave her the sobriquet, half hangit' Maggie. She is purported to have spent the remainder of her long life in the vicinity of the Grassmarket, where for a price, she would recount her story. Noticeable because of her twisted neck, she was said to have directed abuse at the hangman from her open window during subsequent executions. Her home of course was said to have been in the same building as 'Maggie Dickson's' pub. On one occasion, it is said she admonished the executioner in the midst of performing his duties with the immortal words; 'I hope ye dae a better job this time.' This no doubt delighted the crowd though possibly not the condemned, no doubt fervently wishing the opposite. I would like to think this was true.

Our next pub is the Banshee Labyrinth, reputedly the most haunted pub in Scotland, and for once, it's no idle boast. Having visited the establishment recently I was surprised, pleasantly I might add, at the variety of experiences customers and staff have had. These have included poltergeist activity, full figure apparitions, ghostly children and other disconcerting delights. The area steeped in dark history, has no doubt played its part in populating the ether with residual energy, but are there other more potent forces at work? It would seem so, and after a tentative enquiry I was contacted by current staff member Esje. During our conversation, I was hugely impressed by her foresight and fortitude in collating many of her own and her colleagues' experiences. Such diligence is rare, and the material was later used in a podcast by 'Real Life Ghost Stories.'

The building now stands butted against the arches of the South Bridge which I have previously described. On entering, a small bar greets the customer while to the left lies a long narrow seating area. Further on a set of stairs leads down to another seated area. The nearby pool room, which is handily positioned below the South Bridge vaults has unsurprisingly been the location of much unexplained phenomena. Further on sits the famed haunted underground cinema, which is a real coup in my book, and the Mary Queen of Scots room. All are thought to be haunted. There are also numerous toilets, staff rooms and potentially other spaces some of which I have left out. The pub is aptly named. Prior to its renaming it was known as, the 'Nicol Edwards' and the significance of its location goes without saying, being nestled at the foot of haunted Niddry Street. If one believes that energy good or bad can be stored in an area because of past deeds, it is natural to assume that something unpleasant may leave a permanent stain. Perhaps this was the case in the 'Nicol Edwards,' whose namesake resided nearby. He was, some say a despicable man who not only delighted in torturing his wife, but numerous women and was alleged to have kept a secret dungeon below the property. During the darkest years of King James VI reign, hundreds of innocent women and occasionally men, fell victim to the public's bloodlust under the direction of their king. The story goes that Lord Edwards, a confidant of the King was given carte blanche to do as he wished in securing confessions. It was the time of Edinburgh's witch trials and his actions, if true, were more terrifying than any ghost. His house demolished two centuries prior is alleged to have sat on the exact spot, and in it he had his own private torture chamber. It has been suggested he enjoyed getting his hands dirty and begs the question, did he really believe he was doing 'God's work,' or was he a perverted sociopath of the worst kind? The sight of an eyeless woman witnessed during its refurbishment and her subsequent scream, allegedly inspired the name change, though this may be just a story. Stories today include obligatory glass throwing and sightings of shadow figures, but there is more, much more, and so late one afternoon my wife and I duly arrived after being invited to look around. It was still outside opening hours, so this was rare treat indeed and a wonderful opportunity to hear accounts first-hand.

Apparitions such as Old Jock and Molly are two of the most prolific, though there are others, and from other conversations they may not be averse to moving between venues. Jock himself, described as hanging around the ladies' loo is known to take a little too much interest in proceedings though is potentially the least worrying of the ensemble, but I'll let you be the judge.

Our story really kicks off when the pub, newly purchased was being refurbished. The new owner and family were painting downstairs, in what's now known as the Mary Queen of Scots room. It's a large room and much like the rest of the pub is painted black. According to the testimony this was the only time that something had properly freaked him out which I can believe. As they painted, their daughter who was around four appeared preoccupied by something near the door and turning towards her parents asked; 'what does he want?' Who, asked her parents, slightly puzzled by the question? 'The fire ghost,' she replied. Trying to remain calm they then asked, who the fire ghost was, before the girl chillingly replied, 'the man on fire by the door.' Unsurprisingly they took a break.

Our next stop is at the cave bar, described as being the most atmospheric and in which footsteps are heard frequently. I was told that on occasion, it has also served as a place to hunker down for the night, when staff have found themselves stranded. Two members of staff in this instance woke to find a tall dark figure leaning over them, resulting in a sleepless night. Potentially the famed 'watcher' or 'Mr. Boots' if you prefer. This tall dark clad figure in a tricorn hat has been witnessed numerous times in many of the street's pubs and in the adjoining vaults. Described as an imposing figure, who silently observes, and his description has remained constant.

Of course, not all staff members tow the party line and within their ranks, I was told there were a few dissenters. Though no one can deny the feelings of unease that many have described or the sensation of being watched. It's feasible to suggest that perhaps long hours and tiredness may have played its part, and what of the area's history? Perhaps there was a subliminal expectation? One manager no doubt had such thoughts, but they were quickly dispelled on opening one of the back bars. Walking into the darkened bar, he reached for the switch positioned furthest from the door. I can only imagine his surprise on flicking the switch, when confronted by the sight of a man sitting at one of the benches. It was, I was told in the aptly named bar 13, unlucky for some. More alarmingly, I was told that an ex-supervisor and dyed in the wool sceptic, would purposefully antagonise the spirits, challenging them to prove their existence. Obligingly on one shift, he was 'grabbed by his neck and dragged backwards' which I suspect may have given him a change of heart.

It has also been noted that the sound of a male whistling has been frequently heard. Not described as the most tuneful it was heard one evening by Esje, just outside the door of the office where she sat, yet the monitor which she was watching at the time displayed nothing. In case of any doubt my attention was drawn to a CCTV camara positioned outside the office which would have given a clear view of anyone loitering. On that occasion, the monitor at which she sat revealed nothing, yet the whistling continued just outside for some minutes. I must admit I find whistling very annoying at the best of times, but from an unknown source adds a whole new level. It was an unsettling experience, and a medium was eventually called in who on arrival claimed to have contacted a spirit. It was she said, a man who was in the company of several women. Disturbingly she revealed that the women could not leave, being effectively bound to the male. The medium, then went on to say, she could pick up on their misery and fear. She asked if he would let them go? He replied, 'I love each, and every one of them.' The medium was said to have been very disturbed by this revelation.

The phenomena of course, like in all hauntings, abates during periods of respite. But the question remains, what circumstance sets them off again, does it depend on the time of year? Impossible to answer but the following tale, again related by Esje, would suggest it may sometimes be down to the right kind of person. This is what she said. 'One evening an American woman approached the bar and said, I know this sounds crazy, but I think I have something of yours.' A little perplexed, she then listened as the woman explained that a month or so back, she had come in for a drink and on returning home later that evening felt that something had attached itself to her. Esje continued, 'she then told me that in the following days a strange feeling of unease began to come over her and that after a while she began to hear voices in the flat and then poltergeist activity had started up. Being naturally, a little taken a back, I then half-jokingly suggested that the woman should leave it wherever you found it.' The woman apparently placated took her advice and said she would, resulting in an increase of activity within the pub which had been 'quiet,' for the previous month.

On a slightly more comforting note, I was told that not all the spirits are negative, including that of a small girl named Molly. Known to reside in the area, her spirit is as playful as a child's often is. Prone to tug at people's sleeves for attention, she has also been heard running in the corridors and at the bar, where the sound of a young girl's laughter has been detected. One customer witnessed this personally and approached the bar, stating; 'Are you sure you don't allow children in the bar?' The barkeep responding negatively, was then surprised to learn that the customer had just witnessed a small girl walking through a closed gate, leading to the cave bar. The staff member then accompanied the woman back to the area, where they witnessed a very apparent cold spot where the girl had stood. Who was Molly while she was alive is anyone's guess, but it is assumed she was a former resident as during the pub's conversion, a small child's shoe bearing her name was found stuffed up a chimney. During the tour, I had the opportunity to visit the very fireplace myself and I would be lying if said I did not feel a slight tightening of the skin at that point. The pub certainly has an atmosphere not helped by the layout which as the name suggests is labyrinthian. We then returned to the front bar and as it was near opening time, we ordered a drink. It was then Esje asked if we would like to look at a recent photograph of what was suspected to be Molly's handprint. I naturally said yes. On viewing the image revealed a distinct child's handprint on the inside of the pub window, clearly defined against the condensation. I was assured it had not been there when the premises had been locked on the previous evening. The bar also operates a strictly no under eighteens policy, discounting any children being present. I was very impressed.

To add another layer of intrigue, near the end of the tour my wife's phone kept pinging incessantly. Afterwards we calculated around fifteen times, and so wondered who had sent so many texts, on checking we found not one single notification. Ordering drinks, our attention was soon drawn to the bar where a distinct shuffling could be heard which was followed by an audible thump from the next-door bar. The staff were present and exchanged knowing looks. I of course went to look, not wanting to miss a golden opportunity but all was still. It had come from the area next to the chimney. It was at that point, we thought it best to stop discussing Molly.

Soon after I was given the opportunity to interview former staff member Kirsty, who willingly related the following, and is possibly the most detailed account of, 'The Watcher' ever published. This is what she said.

'It would have been around 2007, I had worked at the bar for some time. The cinema part was locked because of water damage and so was unused. Staff would report the sound of giggling coming from this area. We would also frequently have glasses smash spontaneously while sitting untouched on shelves and of course unexplained bangs and crashes were heard from different parts of the bar. Back then the décor was different there were pictures of Mary Queen of Scots on the wall and some of the rooms weren't used during the week as it was quiet. My mum and stepdad both cleaned there so we would often be working together which I was glad of. The female toilets were notorious for strange phenomena, with banging on the cubicle door being reported. I remember one day opening the downstairs bar and I could hear footsteps coming down the stair behind me. Thinking it was my colleague arriving I began talking to them but on getting no reply glanced back, of course there was no one there though I distinctly heard someone enter the room behind me. At other times, staff would hear heavy breathing coming from within locked rooms and we were at times scared to unlock them. Whatever it was of course had by that time gone. One night I had quite a bad experience and to this day think it may have been the Watcher, who I know you have heard of. The incident occurred at the end of the night while I was cleaning glasses in the top bar. It's very small as you know, and the serving hatch is at opposite end to the glasswasher. I was bent over the washer putting the glasses in, when I had a feeling, something was beside me. I glanced back and to the left the first thing I saw was a massive hand. I turned slowly and at the end near the hatch stood a figure. I can describe him today as clearly as I could then, but I can never remember his face, it being indistinct. He was tall and I mean very tall, with massive hands. He had a light shirt on with a ruff at the collar and at the wrists. His hands were enormous and on each finger was a sliver ring. I remember them clearly. They were oval shaped and large. He had long white curly hair and wore a hat. This wasn't like a top hat; it was much shorter but did have a wide brim. He wore a long trench coat and high leather boots. To this day his face, I can't recall. Well, I think I was in shock because I just stood staring and he never moved. I don't know how long it could have been, perhaps five, even ten minutes, but I lost all track of time. It only ended when my colleague, who had been watching on CCTV came into the bar to check on me, and then when I glanced back, the figure had gone. Afterwards I was shaking and demanded to know if he had seen anything, which he hadn't. Strangely the only reason he came down is that he wanted to know what I was doing because all he could see was me staring at an empty space. When we had our usual post work drink, I explained what had happened. They knew I had seen something. I don't know if I would describe the incident as scary, but for some time after I was in shock, anxious at the thought of the figure re-appearing, but thankfully it never did.'

Of all the bars in Edinburgh which claim to be haunted this may be the motherlode and if I haven't persuaded you yet, I will finish with this. In June 2022, while delivering a recent tour I began chatting to a couple from Preston. They were nice folk and during our conversation I recommended that perhaps they should try the Banshee Labyrinth for a drink. They said they might, and we parted ways. The next day, while standing on the Royal Mile I was approached by the same couple who seemed a little animated and it transpired that they had taken my advice on the previous evening and went to the pub. The labyrinth as we have discussed is allegedly haunted by numerous ghosts and being prolific in number, I had neglected to tell them about 'Auld Jock.' Often described as mischievous, he appears to have a penchant for hanging around the toilets and playing tricks on female customers. He has on occasion also been known to try and gain entry to cubicles while in use. The lady of course knew nothing of this until her bag was tugged off her shoulder while at the sink. Assuming at the time, that perhaps it had just slipped, a closer inspection revealed the strap had been unclipped. The clip she told me, does not undo itself and is very hard to remove which she then demonstrated. She went on to say that because of her arthritis her husband must unclip it when needed so whatever had done this, did so instantaneously. On returning to the bar, she explained what had happened which came as no surprise to the staff. On hearing her story, I apologised, perhaps I should stop recommending pubs.

A couple of hundred yards up the street, we reach Whistlebinkies, which with the Banshee Labyrinth and potentially half the premises in the area, share one thing in common, ghosts. Whether 'Bloody George Mackenzie,' 'the Imp' or 'the Watcher,' there appears to be a ghost to suit every occasion, however for now we return to 'the Watcher.' His exploits have featured in many reports and his first appearance, at least within Whistlebinkies pub, was thought to have been around 1994 when he was spotted by the bar designer. The witness described seeing a figure who appeared to be wearing a dress and bravely followed it as it made its way into the cellar. It then vanished abruptly. Afterwards he realised that instead of a dress he had been looking at a figure dressed in an 18th century gentleman's coat.

Back on the Royal Mile and across from Niddry Street, lies the Mitre bar. Built on the site of Archbishop Spottiswoods home who was Lord Chancellor of Scotland during the reign of Charles I, it is yet another traditional pub with a few tales to tell. The pub like so many others is full of both kinds of spirits, and some appear to idle away the hours or possibly centuries, by playing the odd trick. I have often wondered why the spirits are so mischievous, perhaps it is the easiest way to communicate, or maybe they are just bored? Either way, many seem intent on making their presence known by being anti-social and their trickery at the expense of the staff at 'The Mitre' has been well documented. Phenomena has included the obligatory sightings of shadowy figures, appearing in both the bar area and cellar. The old favourite of beer kegs being switched off, has also been reported, a common occurrence in pub hauntings. But who is the ghost? Could it be the spirit of Archbishop Spottiswoode, himself? We do not know but one thing is certain, it is not a music lover as much activity is centred around the jukebox. Take for example the two engineers tasked with installing the machine, who then described being shoved by an invisible entity or the two members of staff working in the cellar after closing time. Alarmed to hear music playing from above they ascended the stairs fearful that someone had broken in, only to find the pub devoid of life while the jukebox kept playing. Assuming, it to be caused by an electrical fault they pulled the plug before heading back downstairs. There are no prizes for guessing what came next, and on investigation the plug was found to be firmly back in the socket. It was at that point they left. Leaving the Mitre, a short ten-minute stagger brings us to the Tolbooth tavern.

The Tolbooth tavern situated at the edge of the Canongate, dates from 1591 and is noted for its striking appearance including its distinctive clock tower, added in 1884. Over the centuries it has been used for both collecting tolls and as a prison. Today on the ground floor sits the titular bar which like many Edinburgh pubs has retained some character and like any self-respecting pub, is allegedly haunted. Sightings have included, dare I say it, shadow figures. Spirits of children have also been reported though what connection they have to the building, is open to question. Staff and customers have also claimed that poltergeist activity happens on occasion, with glasses being moved and pictures being knocked from the walls. Perhaps though there is a more mundane reason for the latter, as recently the very same thing happened in my home, although this proved my DIY skills wanting. There is also rumoured to have been the sighting of spirit prisoners once held in its cells. Historically, Cromwell's forces utilised it, during one of its 'busy periods,' and a subsequent mass breakout resulted in the incarcerated scaling down its frontage with the aid of a blanket while others broke into the lofts of neighbouring buildings. I recently spoke to Heather Burns whose family lived and worked on the Royal Mile for generations, their home being next to the Tolbooth Tavern. During our conversation she described how the iconic street became her playground, including the Canongate churchyard. I can't imagine anything better. Of course, being resident in such an ancient property comes with a price, and the spirits are thought to be of those who escaped. It has been described that on the night of the breakout some prisoners broke through to adjoining properties, escaping into their attics. Heather then revealed that the most frequent phenomena the family witnessed was often the sound of heavy footsteps, heard coming from the attic. I was told that this happened on several occasions despite everyone in the property being accounted for. Similar phenomenon has also been reported in the present-day pub. Heather went on to say that the sound of raised male voices was also commonly heard coming from the Tolbooth after it was closed for the night. A more personal incident was then described as Heather recalled what took place on the day of a family funeral. Sitting afterwards in the Tolbooth tavern, witnesses were shocked to see several books thrown from a nearby case. Heather then said, 'I asked my great aunt to open one of the books and when she did, I found our surname Burns, was written on the inside. Around thirty people bore witness to this. She remains convinced that the tavern is haunted.

Next on our journey is Hunters Tryst, Oxgangs. From the 1980s onwards this ancient hostelry began to hit the headline due to being home to alleged apparitions. Strangely the building which dates from the mid-1700s had acquired a reputation early on, when in use as a farmhouse. The stories which bear all the hallmarks of poltergeist activity came to the public's attention due to the Edinburgh born writer, Robert Louis Stevenson. In 'Edinburgh-Picturesque Notes,' published 1878, Stevenson described hearing of its reputation while staying in the vicinity. The stories being well known locally, were repeated, no doubt with great relish, and Stevenson incorporated some within his book. In it he described the building as being, 'not so long ago haunted by the devil in person.' Whether this was true or not no one can say, however stories regarding invisible agencies throwing plates and objects were common knowledge. Repeating stories, he had heard of including that of a past exorcism, only added to its reputation. A hiatus then followed with little being recorded until more recent times when journalist Rab McNeil took up the baton. An altogether more believable story then unfolded whilst interviewing the current staff. It was in his article that an assistant manager described the following: 'It was like a mist, but you could see the figure but as she had her back to me, I could not see her face. She had a long blue dress on with a bustle at the back. And she wore a small crinoline type of cap. She just floated down the restaurant. I was in the kitchen at the time and saw her move towards the coffee lounge, there was nothing said. I wasn't frightened, there was nothing evil about it. Later, the manager was quoted as saying: 'I felt there was something in the place. The atmosphere would go cold. One Sunday I locked up and took my two dogs for a walk. Suddenly all the lights went on like a Christmas tree.' In case you hadn't guessed, she had switched them off on leaving, and was the only one present. A common problem, staff would invariably have to return after locking up to turn the lights off again though most took it in their stride. The more nervous however would occasionally bring along back up for company. One such 'volunteer,' had second thoughts on experiencing the phenomena for himself, describing the temperature suddenly dropping. He wasted no time in putting the light off and on leaving they sprang on again. Mustering his courage, he then reopened the building and flicked the switch again, this time deciding not to look back on his departure. Whatever is present in the building however is not thought to be dangerous or vindictive, just playful as many spirits seem to be. Perhaps it is one of their only means of communication and therefore we must be forgiving of their peccadillos?

And so, as we finish our pub crawl it is worth pointing out that our list is not exhaustive, there being many others that enliven the city. The casual tourist can potentially trip over them in the Old Town, however further afield other gems await discovery. Having not had the time to investigate further, I will point out a few that may be of interest. Heading towards the New Town for example, on Northumberland Place, sits the Star Bar. This might be of particular interest for those interested in curses. Perhaps a niche market I realise, but the bars main claim to fame is that it contains a human skull. This grisly relic apparently found during excavations, is according to the owners cursed and when touched or removed has led to a series of misfortunes. Apparently, this is a real thing thus the skull has become permanent resident. The Golf Tavern near Bruntsfield links is another. Allegedly the haunt of a Victorian gentleman he has been seen both inside and outside of the establishment. I have little detail yet, but a former worker who I spoke to briefly, said she had witnessed the apparition some years back. There are of course many others, but the stories are so fragmented, and half whispered it is difficult to ascertain whether some have just jumped on the ghostly bandwagon. For me though, my money remains on the Banshee Labyrinth, I felt a presence there as did my wife, and that's good enough for me.

Haunted Hotels: Room with a Boo

T he weary traveller in hope of a good night's rest after traversing the many closes and stairs of Auld Reekie may wish to take note of the following. Edinburgh's ghosts are night owls and judging by the number of after-hours activities witnessed in the city, they are busy. Some spirits as we have seen are still attached to favoured city watering holes, but as we shall now see others prefer the comfort of a good hotel. A quick glance in this section will reassure those of nervous disposition of which to avoid, however if you are already there and while reading make a startling discovery, I apologise. Like pubs there are many hotels which by all accounts are hot beds, literally, of spiritual activity. Some are new while others have an older pedigree, but the commonality is that they are frequented by shadows from the past. The wealthy however can rest easy as one of the few escapees appears to be 'The Balmoral,' a hotel so expensive that even ghosts can't afford the tariff. Of course, while staying in Edinburgh, the sighting of a ghost is not guaranteed though many would be pleased to have that experience, case in point, being a recent article in the Edinburgh Evening news. The article devoted to the bizarre requests that staff have been asked for, was certainly an eye-opener and incredible as it seems they were all true. My personal favourite involved a family staying at the Rose Street Travelodge who enquired at reception, if the hotel staff could arrange for their family to meet the ghosts living in the haunted vaults. I wonder what the receptionist thought. Not satisfied with repeating some of the better-known stories concerning the city, though I have done so in some instances, I searched high and low for the slightly more obscure. In one such trawl I came across a spooky forum, the thread being haunted hotels. It was an enlightening read and one such hotel was The Apex, situated in the Grassmarket. Of course, being a relatively new building purists may blanche at the idea of ghosts in such a contemporary setting. It does however sit on ancient land and judging by what was witnessed, the spirits, which are plentiful appear to have been former residents of the Grassmarket, once one of the most poverty-stricken areas in the city.

Here is a selection of recent gems, which may or may not increase footfall in the above establishment. Around three years ago one visitor reported being woken up on their first night, only to witness a man with a dark coat sitting on the edge of her bed. He vanished before her eyes making for a very restless night. It must have been with some trepidation that they looked forward to their second night which as it turned out was even worse. In this instance she was rudely woken by her arm being squeezed tightly, and on springing awake saw nothing. I found out later that a year prior to this, another guest had been woken in the wee small hours, by the presence of a screaming man. The experience by all accounts left the resident terrified. She described him clearly, as a man; 'with lots of facial hair and dirty clothing.' She went on to say that his hair was dark, but whether through dirt or colouring she could not ascertain. Standing next to him was a woman dressed in grey. She was noted to be wearing a white hat and apron (perhaps a servant?) and stood wringing her hands. Afterwards the guest found out that in the past the area had been used for executions, which she felt may have accounted for what she was witnessed. Hangings of course, were a regular occurrence in the Grassmarket. Other guests in the ensuing years have had similarly eventful stays with one stating; 'It was the worst night of my life; I felt a horrible feeling of dread all night.' Another report stated. 'On the first night we stayed, there were footsteps in our room near to our beds and then someone stood watching.' I hope to God they didn't leave a review on trip advisor.

Another contributor went as far as to mention the actual room, being on the 2nd floor, and stated, 'I had the same experience (the footsteps round the bed) The television kept turning on and off and I saw a shadow move along the side of my bed. There was nothing fun about it. I told the reception, and they told me they had heard the story before.' Following on from these which I concede would be terrifying if experienced first-hand, I found something a little more amusing. It came courtesy of Trip Advisor and though it was a great review, it was a little sparing in its detail. The review was headed 'Excellent Hotel,' and read thus: 'I loved the hotel. The only thing is that I was scared by a ghost. But I think it is part of Edinburgh experience. The breakfast is amazing.' The manager then replied: 'It was great you had such a nice stay.' I applauded his successful navigation of the ghost issue, and if I were him, I would consider a career in the field of diplomacy.

Other hotels nearby suspected to be haunted include Grass market Hotel, though I have nothing to offer other than generic descriptions. Perhaps though the most terrifying part of the Grassmarket is the ensuing carnage that take place every weekend as numerous hen and stag parties invade the area. These make ghosts the least of our worries. Yet looking beyond the deep-fried mars bars, screaming drunks, and poor manners, you will find an area steeped in history. It goes without saying that most sightings occur in the wee small hours, the 'deid ceilings of the night,' as travellers described it, a time when the veneer between this world and the next was at its thinnest. At this time, when the last drunks have staggered home, and quiet has descended, the sound of horse's hoofs on cobbles have been heard while some have claimed to have heard children singing nursery rhymes. It has without doubt, a certain atmosphere.

Speaking of hotels, lets revisit our old friend Niddry Street so overpopulated with ghosts its almost embarrassing and our destination now is the Radisson Blu. Perhaps due to its proximity to the site of 'Bloody' George Mackenzie's former home it too has had its share of paranormal activity. Well documented fires have broken out in the area for decades, and indeed its predecessor the Scandic and Crowne Plaza both allegedly were prone to the odd conflagration. Some have even the suggested the devastating fire that took place in nearby Cowgate some years back was somehow tied in with this. It is more than likely down to faulty wiring; however the area does appear to have had more than its fair share. As three hotels have operated on basically the same spot in recent years, its perhaps best that we start with the latest incarnation the Radisson and work our way backwards. The current hotel like its predecessors does appear to be prone to several unquiet spirits, creating likewise unquiet nights for unsuspecting guests. Take for example the following contributor who recently stayed on the 3rd floor of the Radisson and was hardly able to sleep a wink when she kept hearing a little girl giggling in the bathroom. 'I felt I was being watched from the moment I arrived,' she later stated. She then reported her experience to the receptionist, who appeared nonplussed. Pity the ghost whose appearance garners less fuss than a dirty cup. One must assume by the staff reaction that perhaps these complaints aren't that uncommon. There have of course been many other sightings over the years, and it is commonly thought to be a haunted hotel. This of course doesn't dissuade guests and in fact may encourage some. Most spirits however appear content to haunt at a respectful distance. On that note I don't believe for a minute that spirits are out to get us, in fact if anything we should be more afraid of the living, but perhaps it's the way some spirits present themselves that's most unnerving. This is particularly true of those spirits thought to be connected to the time of the great plague, whose ragged forms have been described within the hotel. Reports vary, and there are a few, but the most common appear to describe very distinct apparitions. One witness in the lower part of the hotel for example claimed to have seen a group of people sitting in the middle of the laundry room. They were described as wearing 'old, tatty clothes', and vanished before the startled witnesses' eyes. Who they were, and what bizarre tableaux was being played out remains a mystery. It has been suggested they could have been plague victims, but as there is no further description it's difficult to say. As a citizen of modern-day Edinburgh, I am aware of the layers of history in that area and so potentially there could be any number of spirits from differing eras. The question is, are they aware of each other? I like to think so. More difficult to reconcile is a situation when the spirit you stumble across reacts to your presence as in the case of a former employee, Angus Grant. He claimed to have had similar experience while making his rounds. At the time of the incident, it was noted as being early in the morning at around 3am. He described doing a security check and in doing so got out of the lift on the 1st floor. Ahead of him sat a 'ragged girl,' outside one of the rooms, who on noticing him leapt to her feet and ran. After the initial shock, he bolted after her and turning the corner where she had just turned, he was met with nothing. According to his account he manfully continued his rounds and for this display of fortitude, I tip my hat.

Our next destination is Morrison Links and The Leonardo Royal. Formerly the Travelodge, it is a relatively new build and sits near Haymarket Station. It is yet another example of why a cleaner's lot is a tough one and in a recent conversation, housekeeper Geri Milne, described why both she and her colleagues believe the building to be haunted. Only recently finding out one rooms history.

During one conversation a colleague alluded to an unfortunate incident which occurred some ten years prior in which a guest took his life. The manner of his passing, suffice to say was not pleasant and his subsequent discovery the next day by two housekeepers was so traumatic it prompted both to return to their native France. Since then, if the story is to be believed, and it does seem to be genuine, numerous workers have described feeling a very heavy and ominous vibe in the room and a feeling of being watched. Strangely this unpleasant atmosphere is not confined to the second-floor room but also to those adjacent and on the floors directly above and below, suggesting the grim chain of events has left an indelible mark. This makes rota time, a time of anxiety. Geri went on to describe that on more than one occasion she was convinced there was someone standing behind her whilst cleaning and on one occasion distinctly heard someone say the word 'hello,' in her ear. Not a place for the faint hearted.

Of course, once the cat was out of the bag as it were, colleagues began to discuss their own experiences and unsurprisingly many had a tale to tell. Among the numerous examples, includes the sighting of a figure entering a nearby room. Witnessed by Victoria, she then knocked on the door, to ascertain their reason for being there. She received no answer and on entering found the room to be empty. On another occasion staff heard conversations coming from a room, punctuated by the distinct sound of laughter. Again, the housekeeper knocked and despite repeated attempts, received no answer. In frustration she then phoned reception for advice only to find the room remained un-booked.

A further conversation revealed that despite the second floors reputation, other areas are not completely devoid of phenomena. Take for example the staff seating area, where documents, bags and other personal items have been found strewn on the floor. A quick conversation revealed that no one from the night team had used the space which made it difficult to ascertain the strewn belongings. Another recent example involved one worker arriving early for her shift who described hearing voices coming from the office. She initially assumed it to be her supervisor however the sound abruptly stopped on her knocking. Perplexed as to why she had not answered the door, a further knock, again elicited no reply. To her surprise her manager duly arrived sometime later apologising for her lateness, having been held up. The office was then opened to reveal nothing. Despite this some have suggested that perhaps co-workers have exaggerated events or perhaps even fabricated the stories? This however does not explain the frequently heard disembodied voices which even management have borne witness to. With over two hundred rooms, the hotel copes with a massive number of guests and in doing so one expects the energy may not always be good. If the fate of that visitor is true, then perhaps a negative residual energy remains?

The former Learmonth hotel located around two minutes from my current flat is also conveniently about a minutes' walk from the 'Mummy's Curse,' house. This of course, makes my locale a very spooky one indeed. I often used to pass by this former hotel and would on occasion ruminate on its supposed haunting. On passing, I would afford myself a glance at its windows. They of course gave nothing away, remaining resolutely blank. Not so long ago, I toyed with the idea of renting a room there just to see but as the building is now used to house refugees, that is now impossible. In Scottish Ghosts by Lily Seafield, she describes how the resident spirit appears to like playing pranks in typical poltergeist fashion. This includes opening doors and locking people out of their rooms. Not the most exciting phenomena for any ghost obsessive you would agree, possibly being more likely a case of dodgy locks. Still, I like to keep an open mind and delving further I was rewarded by a recent review in Trip Advisor which gave me some hope. The heading read, Ghosts???, and on further scrutiny it turned out to be a 3-star review. The author was named Eleanor, a resident of Havant, whose deadpan delivery made me chuckle. Of course, I am not sure how many stars were devoted to either the quality of the room, its cleanliness or the ghost, but I don't suppose it matters. The review read. 'Not a particularly great hotel, good location, comfortable bed. Grandson was suddenly turfed out of bed during the night so there may well be some truth in the ghost stories. He said it felt like someone just lifted the bed. I can certainly verify he landed on the floor with a bang. The bar staff seemed more interested in cashing up to change over shifts.' Perhaps it had been a long day.

Other supposed haunted hotels include the Howard on Great King Street and the Royal Circus, both thought to have respective female spirits. They however seem unobtrusive in their meanderings, making the odd appearance being the sum of their haunting. In desperation I began to trawl various databases in the hope of finding new leads. As both hotels are frequently mentioned I had assumed there would be more to the stories attached, but no, I had come to a dead end. The problem, I realised is our reliance on the web which tends to showcase well known stories, a good proportion of which are summarised. Databases are like trawlers they can catch a huge haul, irrespective of whether they are edible or not subsequently leaving researchers swimming in a sea of vagueness, if you forgive further water analogies. One did catch my attention though, and I must admit it made me laugh. The location, barely hinted at, allegedly took place in a private house in the 1970's. On reading I quickly realised how sparing in detail it was. Further on though I discovered there was mention of a supposed phantom monk which according to the owner was apparently friendly, and he asked people not to scream if they saw it.

Ghosts Galore

As mentioned, I've always had a fascination with the supernatural and as a kid enjoyed nothing better than a good, Fontana Ghost Book or Pan Book of Horror. I avidly devoured their contents and for my sins suffered the odd sleepless night. I had of course my favourites and without question was always drawn to those who wrote classic ghost stories. At the age of twenty-one however an incident occurred that made me realise that not all spectral activity was confined to the yellowing pages of those paperbacks. Let me set the scene.

I had just started a relationship, doomed to end quickly but at the time assumed it was the beginning of a great romance. I was convinced that the poets of the future would look to it for inspiration. She had, literally within weeks of our meeting moved to Dunfermline, though had not yet moved into the property. The house now empty, had once belonged to the church of Scotland, and her family had opted to do the necessary repairs before moving in. This meant a few weeks living out of suitcases at a five-star hotel on Lothian Road. Her father's company was footing the bill, so there was no issue there, however she had neglected to tell him of my proposed visit. On arrival I was mortified to learn the truth and I remember clearly the audible conversation which ensued. Her father made no attempt to lower his tones, and on remerging from the bedroom tossed me a sleeping bag. I had, as it transpired, been volunteered to do a little house-sitting in Dunfermline and so accepting the responsibility with good grace. An interminable drive then followed before we reached the outskirts of Dunfermline and our destination. The house was large and gloomy, and on inspection devoid of furniture. Thankfully the lights worked and once switched on I was able to see the large central staircase and off it several large rooms. With little ceremony I was ushered to the right where her father indicated I should make myself comfortable. I unfurled my sleeping bag and after a few 'pleasantries' he wished me adieu before hightailing it back to luxury. There was not a stick of furniture on which to relax and still being relatively early, I sat smoking pondering the vicissitudes of romance. To this day can't remember what time it was when I eventually settled down, but I recall sitting against the wood panelling encased in the sleeping bag. Outside there sat a large overgrown hedge and beyond it a streetlight which afforded me some partial light. And it was in this setting I eventually dozed off. Sometime later, though I cannot recall the time, I was awoken abruptly by something grabbing both my ankles. A second later my head clattered off the wooden floor, and I was awake. It took mere seconds to struggle out of the bag and when I did, I found I was sitting three feet from the wall. What had pulled me, I have no idea, but I was scared. Nothing like this had happened before, and nothing since, but the sensation of being grabbed was physical, much as if a living person had done the deed. I was certain I hadn't slid accidently and after a few minutes' further contemplation, made a dash for the switch just inside the door. Light flooded the room and I quickly retreated to my rucksack, where I smoked the first of many cigarettes. When the light of dawn crept over the hedge, I must have felt safe enough to afford some rest and soon dozed off. Some hours later I was wakened by my hosts'. I did not mention what happened for fear of ridicule. The feeling of being bodily pulled across that floor has stuck with me for over thirty years, and I am in no doubt what took place was of paranormal origin. Further visits remained free of incident, soon after our relationship ended, proving there's nothing like a ghost story with a touch of pathos.

Ghosts of course do not just frequent the Old Town and in a city teeming with alleged supernatural occurrences one does not have to look far. For our next venture we will look at several locations across the city. I am pleased to say that many will be new to readers and add to Edinburgh's supernatural canon. So, our first stop we take a short walk along to the east end of Princes Street, to Waterloo place. Ahead in the distance looms Calton Hill, with its magnificent one-sided Parthenon, known locally as Edinburgh's shame. Continuing around the base of the hill you eventually reach Regent Terrace, one of the city's most prestigious streets which on viewing is easy to see why. A Georgian street, it is now home to several consulates however in 1978 things were a little different. The city then was a little rougher around the edges, the explosion in tourism still some way off and though there was still old money, there were also areas of dilapidation. Regent Terrace was one such place. Yes, there were expensive houses, but scattered between were many run-down properties, flats that only students would take or those on lower incomes. It was in one of those the following events unfolded. A particularly unpleasant experience for those involved it took place at number 25 to be precise and the entity became known, unsurprisingly, as the Regent Terrace poltergeist.

Recalled in an old issue of the 'Fortean Times' the basement home was described at the time as being damp and gloomy. The occupants consisted of one female and three males one of whom was Bill Gibbons who contributed the story. Soon after moving in, and knowing nothing of its history, the new occupants began to hear a baby crying which would get increasingly louder before stopping abruptly. They discovered later of course that there were no families with children living in the vicinity. Soon afterwards, Bill stated that one day while filling the kettle, a loud voice 'barked in his ear,' the word 'yes.' Shocking as it was it was exacerbated by the sight of their pet cat which then cowered and hissed from beneath the sink. But worse was to follow.

A flatmate then woke to find the bed vibrating alarmingly before something heavy and furry leapt onto it. As if that was not enough, the sound of his own cat now hissing in terror, outside the bedroom was the clincher. Afterwards he persuaded the males to move their beds into one room. Soon after when they had a guest stay over, things got decidedly worse. Clicking the light off the room was plunged into darkness and as they settled down something thought to be their cat, launched itself onto one of the beds. The unlucky recipient now stroking its furry body began talking to it soothingly before being admonished by the rest. Who was he talking too, they enquired? Somewhat taken aback he replied it was the cat. How could it be, demanded a chorus of nervous voices? For each claimed to have the cat on their own bed! A fumbling hand then switched on the light to reveal four startled faces and a deficit of cats. Unsurprisingly three of the occupants moved out soon after. Bill remained, though now in the process of organising a flat share with his upstairs neighbour, he intended to move out as soon as viable.

Soon after, the now lone tenant described a further incident more terrifying than before. Occurring while reaching for his bedside light his wrist was grabbed by something he described as wet and furry, the resulting shock sending him upstairs to seek company. He later claimed that while looking back as he ran upstairs, he saw what he described as a pair of slitted yellow eyes, glaring balefully at him out of the darkness. Naturally he vacated the flat soon afterwards and the 'haunting' remains unresolved. Was it the ghost of a cat or something darker? We will never know, but if four people were convinced that something evil had taken up residence and was enough to drive them away, then it must have been bad. I suspect their poor cat, who on more than one occasion seemed beside itself with fear must have been heartily relieved to leave also. Pets, they suggest, are much more sensitive to energy and are perhaps aware of the things we pass unwittingly. What do they see, I often wonder? Perhaps it's best not to know?

Opposite Regents Terrace sits St Andrew House built on the site of the Old Calton gaol which housed some of the city's most dangerous prisoners. These include one William Burke, body snatcher/murderer. The building long demolished has left a few reminders of its presence including the governor's house which still sits opposite on Calton Hill. Another reminder though admittedly less noticeable is the door of its condemned cell now residing in the Beehive pub on the Grassmarket. Also mercifully hidden are the bodies of the ten murderers who met their end within the prison and who are now buried beneath the west wing of the current carpark. These include John Henry Savage, Philip Murray, Patrick Wiggins and baby farmer Jessie King, the last woman to be hanged in Edinburgh. Elizabeth Williams an employee in

1969 recounted. 'I worked in the registry in the basement of St. Andrews House for a couple of months and was scared witless by the messengers, who delighted in telling me about the ghosts of the prisoners who had died at Calton jail, that haunted the basement. I never saw anything but quickly joined in the telling of the same stories to new starts.' Unfortunately, stories from this location are a little thin on the ground, but it certainly has the right credentials, with people claiming to have heard unexplained voices coming from the oldest parts of the building.

Our next tale takes us to Walker Street in the cities west end and proves that not all spirits are out to cause mischief or harm. In this instance, John McCutcheon who was studying drama at the Edinburgh Acting School in 1985, had a surprising but positive encounter. He takes up the story. 'I remember one night I couldn't sleep and sat upright in bed. I saw a blueish tinge round the door. It then began to cross the room and came nearer to my bed. It was then I started to see an image. I was scared but not in panic. The image became clearer, and I saw this man standing at the foot of the bed with a walking stick. I was worried, but for some reason I could not say anything. There was no hostility in this man, and he looked kind. He was there for about five seconds then just left through the door. It was about two weeks later I saw my landlady and I asked her if there was a ghost. She just looked at me and smiled and asked what I had seen. I explained everything about this man, how he was dressed, the walking stick and there was a sweet smell. She paused and smiled and said that must have been husband. She said he must have come to see you, to tell you something or show you something. I then said, I had no idea what that might be. She then took me into the hall where there was a locked cupboard and brought out trays of the most beautiful butterflies I have ever seen. Her husband had collected them, and she had not opened the cupboard in twelve years. I was stunned, but at my young age did not appreciate enough to understand. I never saw him again and I moved out 3 months later. I will always treasure my time there; it was a beautiful flat, so much warmth and character. I sometimes wonder if he pops back but I know his wife is probably with him now. I have no idea what would have happened to the butterfly collection, it was stunning.

Our next destination and a little more disturbing, is Wauchope graveyard where in 1962 Ian Suggitt had an encounter he has never forgotten. He contacted me recently and passed on the following. 'I used to spend Friday evening at my girlfriends, now wife's house, in Niddrie Mains Drive. I lived in the prefabs in Greendykes Terrace, and a walk home took me about twenty-five minutes on the long route, but if it was a moonlit night, I could take a short cut through the Wauchope woods. This saved me about ten minutes which I did on this night. As I approached the old Wauchope graveyard, which was beside a tin gate, I could see quite clearly what looked like a woman dressed in a long black dress of yesteryear, just standing with her back to me. She was standing right next to a huge tree. I thought it was strange for a woman to be out on her own at this time, being about 12.30am, so I started whistling as I approached so as not to alarm her. As I approached what happened next scared the living daylights out of me, she seemed to swivel her head round 90 degrees without moving her body, and the ghostliest white face with staring eyes looked straight at me. Well, I took off like a scalded cat and reached the tin gate in record time, running home without looking back. The strange thing is, when I got home, my mother said, you look like you have seen a ghost. I never told her what happened, and I never took that shortcut again. If I was of an artistic bent, which I am not, I could draw this scene time after time, as it is still fresh in my mind as if it was yesterday.'

Our next tale is of the more vintage variety and occurred in Blackett Place, near Prestonfield, in 1871 to be precise. First recorded by a Mrs Breitzcke in 1886, being an associate of the Society for Physical Research, it describes a frightening and prolonged encounter. The MacMurdo family and their four daughters, Misses, P, K, E and Z, were the main protagonists and it was their testimony which formed the bulk of the report. The phenomena reportedly lasted around seven years. Strangely, although all four girls were witness to extreme experiences, they were reticent to claim their house was haunted, instead believing their imagination had played tricks upon them. Various reasons have been offered up to explain the phenomena, including the pervading damp conditions and indigestion. I wonder where I have heard that before? The detail of the exact location remains elusive to this day, and at the time, as a mark of respect, the account was not published till some fifteen years later. It is however regarded as being an authentic tale and their testimony full of detail, impressed the society. The first to witness the apparition was one of the occupants' daughters, who described the figure as that of a woman, dressed in white. Typically, over time the sightings became a regular occurrence with the figure being seen frequently on the staircase. Neglecting to tell anyone of her experience, this is what she said. 'I saw the figure of a woman about medium size, standing on about the fourth step from the bottom, she had her arms folded and was draped all over in white, her head included. She seemed to be watching me.' The girl, in her terror then ran into the nearby schoolroom, returning moments later, having persuaded herself it had, 'been a fancy,' only to find the apparition had disappeared. Perhaps through embarrassment, the family remained blissfully unaware of the unfolding events until their other daughter's experience, witnessing a similar figure while ascending the staircase, she described her as a tall woman, transparent, who looked at her for few seconds before turning into the passageway that led to the bathroom. She went on to say, 'not knowing what it was, I had not the slightest fear.' A subsequent search of the bathroom again revealed nothing.

The sightings now become more frequent, a further appearance taking place in their mother's bedroom, again the recipient her daughter, stated, 'it stood with arms folded looking straight at me, with a most heartbroken expression in her eyes, even at first glance it did not look real, as the dark blue curtain was visible all through it, but less so at the face and shoulders.' The figure again vanished at which point the girl became frightened. The family stoically carried on and one gets the impression, they accepted their uninvited guest without too much issue. Certainly, the apparition's melancholic demeanour inspired pity more than fear, however soon after things became a shade darker. On this occasion one of the girls having been asked to go to the attic, was fetching some wine. Having completed the task, the household was then disturbed by a terrific crash and on investigating found their sibling lying unconscious at the foot of the stairs. Around her lay the remains of the wine bottle. Her sister then noticed the same wan figure standing above in her usual spot and concluded, the girl had fainted on seeing her. She was however surprised to learn upon her sister's recovery the truth of the matter, a sharp blow from the ghostly assailant being the cause. No longer assumed to be a friendly ghost, the family were no doubt anxious and phenomena such as cold other-worldly hands touching at their heads, were now felt regularly. Another staircase appearance soon followed this time causing the cook, who was carrying hot water bottles, to fall resulting in a badly burned arm.

Then one evening while the house was near empty and the family attending a concert, a second visitor from beyond paid a visit. This time there was no mistaking its intent, and unlike before convinced the family there was something malevolent afoot. The remaining occupants described as being the eldest and youngest daughter, were fast asleep initially before the eldest awoke abruptly. There was something in the room, something intangible and with it came a feeling of dread which slowly enveloped her. On glancing around, it was then she noticed she had uninvited company in the shape of a sinister apparition. She stated: 'just appearing around the door, of a cupboard, was the face of a man, the most wicked and evil looking face. I have ever seen, more like a demon's face than anything else. The skin was a yellowy colour and it had black hair, moustache, and beard.' Most frighteningly was its apparent ability to elongate, the head being described as stretching round the corner and exposing its neck. Transfixed in fear she sat frozen for around quarter of an hour before the face, still regarding her with the intent of a snake, slowly withdrew. Terrified, she was greatly relieved on the return of her family, the subsequent search gleaning nothing, the cupboard being too small to contain a person. Afterwards further noise plagued the house including what they called, the 'morning bang,' always at 6am, and with the regularity of an alarm. Strange noises akin to the rustling of dried leaves, the sound of footsteps and their names being called from an empty room, were all described to the society. Whether a full-blown investigation ever took place, I cannot say, however the incidents were deemed authentic enough for them to take note. Recently I inadvertently found myself on the very street and walked along it, thinking of this story and from which house it came. The spirit, at least the female one, was allegedly linked to a suicide in the property some years prior but in typical fashion the story remains open ended.

Now we arrive at Tolcross, home to a former nightclub Coasters, where Clubgoers once had a choice of three different areas within the premises. These consisted of the Outer Limits on the ground floor, the Bermuda Triangle on the second and above it the Barbados Suite. The year was 1989, and at the time the club had garnered a reputation as being haunted. The story, then featured in the local paper, was soon followed by several follow up articles. It was an ongoing saga; the readers at one point being left tantalised by the proposed visit of a trance medium. If this took place however, I do not know. It was without a doubt, a well-documented case at the time and with several witnesses happy to recount their experiences remains a credible example. Typically, cleaners took most of the brunt with much of the activity described as centring around the Barbados suite. The varied phenomena included the sighting of a vacuum cleaner which 'danced by itself' when unplugged and in the morning those first in frequently reported finding broken glasses strewn on the floor. There were also sightings of a figure on the premises and random puddles of water would manifest, making staff anxious. On January the 2nd of the same year, while the premises were closed for a holiday, neighbours reportedly heard a terrified woman's screams coming from the night club. So real was the incident that several people attempted to gain access assuming something dreadful was taking place. The investigation which followed, found it to be empty.

Afterwards, three cleaners who regularly worked there, were interviewed. One described sitting in the Bermuda Triangle, during their break, when the sight of an apparition appeared in a nearby mirror. Mrs Hetty Graham elaborated, stating that 'the figure was drifting back and forwards, then suddenly it just went away,' she bolted from the room, terrified, her feet barely touching the stairs. Her workmate, Tina Stewart, then spoke of a time when the vacuum cleaner began moving around the floor on its own. Perhaps the spirits energy was drawn to electricity or maybe some have a fascination with modern appliances? Manager Rick Protheroe, no doubt au fait with the goings on offered his own theory, suggesting that perhaps the ghost was that of a girl thought to have died in a fire on the premises. The reporter of course, and rightly so, followed this up, only to be told, that although a fire did occur in 1932 there had been no fatalities. Eventually a psychic was called in who claimed to have identified the spirit, being that of a young man. He was, according to her, earthbound and trapped within the building though who he was remained unclear.

Not long after another similar story appeared in the paper, this time from nearby 'Tokyo Joes,' situated in Home Street. Conveniently for the ghost, it was found to sit back-to-back with the 'Outer Limits.' Having been destroyed by fire, just prior to the initial article being published, the manager was keen to share their experiences, stating, the haunting was common knowledge among the staff and that sightings of a tall man in a cape had been witnessed. One staff member reportedly said, 'we sometimes held seances after the bar had shut and all sorts would happen, including stools that would move,' quite common after a good scare I would imagine. On reading further I discovered similar phenomena had been reported to that of its neighbour, which begs the question, could it have been the same spirit? Sometime later a reader contacted the paper and put forward her own theory suggesting the spirit might have been that of a young lad who disappeared from Morrison Street during the second war. Why she suggested this, was never elaborated.

Heading further back in time to 1957, readers of the Evening Despatch, were astonished to read a series of reports, of 'strange happenings in a city council house.' This headline referred to an outburst of alleged poltergeist activity, which subsequently became one of the most well documented cases in Scotland, the location 5 Hazeldean Terrace. Synonymous with poltergeist activity to this day, it is still regarded as a classic haunting and the fact it lasted nigh on six years makes it one of the longest running cases ever recorded. Home to a Mr and Mrs Currie, at the time of the incident, they appeared happy to recount their experiences of 'living with a ghost' in several articles. Surprisingly, I found that after the initial flurry of activity, there had been a hiatus of almost four years before the papers returned. Even more surprising was the phenomena had never ceased during their absence.

I soon discovered that much of the initial activity took place around the kitchen. These along with bathrooms are usually regarded as the most haunted rooms, so this was unsurprising. There are many theories as to why this might be the case, the most popular being running water attracts energy. Statistically speaking there are more paranormal occurrences recorded on rainy nights, than at any other time. As

Scotland in general suffers from poor weather, perhaps this may explain why we have such a proliferation of ghosts. Anyhow the story quickly became big news and the reporter showing true dedication to his calling opted to stay over as the tenant's guest. His articles later described several regular occurrences, much of which centred around the sink. He noted that a wooden sink cover was for example thrown onto the floor quite regularly, though on first moving in he was told it used to happen daily. It was known to make a thunderous crash as if thrown by force. Other phenomena of the classic poltergeist kind then ensued, leaving a trail of broken glasses, gramophone records and crockery for the homeowners to deal with. Mrs Currie stoically remarked, 'I used to go to bed at night and leave these things in the kitchen, when I came down in the morning they were broken. Peculiarly the tumbler, a thick Jacobean type was not smashed to pieces on the kitchen floor but rather lay in two halves. Three years ago, it was more frightening.'

On another occasion a different reporter was given permission to say over and again recorded hearing loud crashes from the kitchen during the night. When they investigated later, the room was found to be undisturbed. Mrs Currie, later stated, 'The noise and breaking of crockery is less frequent now, maybe once a month or sometimes twice. I just take it as it comes. Apart from the continual breaking of my China, it does us no harm. I prefer not to meddle with spirits and things I do not understand.' Six years later, the story like the phenomena eventually fizzled out, leaving us to speculate if it still occurs today.

Now across town, we pay a visit to Dean Park Cemetery, childhood playground of Angela Fotheringham who in the

1950s was a regular visitor, that is until…… well I will let her words speak from themselves. In her statement, she described spending many happy days exploring the area, including the 'Polish Church' and the churchyard where they would root amongst the statues and catacombs. Running amongst the headstones one day and in her excitement, Angela found herself separated from her companions. Now heading towards one of the archways within the cemetery she then passed by a marble statue which she described as being either Christ or an angel.' As she passed, she was startled to feel a cold hand placed upon her shoulder. Not waiting to see who had touched her she flew home in terror. Afterwards and in the ensuing days she was haunted, for the want of a better word, by the sensation of a hand on her shoulder. She told me this remained constant whether at home, in class or in bed. Some nights after, she awoke suddenly to find a figure sitting at the end of the bed. I asked her what it had looked like, and she replied, 'she thankfully couldn't see it.' The figure then let out a sigh before vanishing. After dozing off she was relieved to find that on wakening the strange sensation on her shoulder had gone. She described to me that it was an incident that has stuck in her mind despite the intervening years. A sceptic of course might argue it was all down to childhood imagination, but what if it was not?

Nearby Inverleith park also claims its fair share of ghosts, with two children being seen in the vicinity wearing old-fashioned clothing. Reports date back to the 1950s and there have been successive sightings in each of the following decades, but the question of who they are remains elusive. A recent post on YouTube, by North Edinburgh Nightmares (well worth a watch) suggests that the boys may not be content to stay within the confines of the park having potentially been seen in nearby Comely Bank Road. The owners of a property on the road, who at the time were busy washing their windows, were interrupted in their toil when two boys passing by stopped to chat to them. Being polite, the homeowners reciprocated. Moments later, on stepping inside to retrieve water, the householder was shocked to witness the boys disappearing, as he watched them through the window. His partner still outside remained unaware of their disappearance and carried on with a very one-side conversation. Moments later she was surprised to learn that they no longer stood behind her. It was only in conversation afterwards that they both realised how odd the boys clothing appeared, being Tweed. Now I know what you are thinking, its Comely Bank, but I can assure readers despite its middle-class image most residents appear to prefer sportswear. In the aftermath, their experience was described as more perplexing rather than scary. Soon after a flurry of comments asserted that sightings of the boys were well known in the area, some having been seen as long ago as the 1950s. Details remain scant despite this.

Moving further afield, we next look at the possible sighting of a monk. Monks are a great favourite of mine, having explored their many appearances over the years. As ghosts go, they look the part being both cowled and silent and pop up in all manner of places. Pubs, private homes, parks, they are prolific in their meanderings. Mainly witnessed in areas where places of worship once stood, they're one of the most witnessed apparitions and Edinburgh is no exception. From the Royal Mile to Holyrood Palace, they have habitually, ahem, been witnessed. The following account was provided by John, who had a surprising encounter one evening while out walking with his partner near Ravenscroft farm. Ravenscroft which lies between Gilmerton Dyes and Station Road was an area they knew well and so they were taken aback to suddenly hear children's voices. Stopping momentarily, he listened intently only to discover that voices appeared to be singing, 'ring a roses.' Seeking reassurance from his partner he was stunned to realise that she had heard nothing. Perplexed they began to walk with more purpose and very soon had turned the corner which led towards their path home. It was there, that around twenty -five feet ahead of them stood a hooded figure. Described as being well over six feet tall, it never moved, and the couple now rooted to the spot could only stare. A quick glance revealed it to be a monk and as their eyes travelled down its body, they noticed it did not have any feet. What should they do, the path home now lay ten yards nearer the figure? John explained that to this day he remains unsure what broke the spell, but within seconds his wife had bolted ahead quickly took the path home. John, momentarily undecided then followed. I can only imagine the conversation that took place once safely home. After much persuasion they retraced their route the following night. This time however they found nothing, other than the five-bar gate, by which the figure had stood on the previous evening.

Moving on to the west end we arrive at Charlotte Square one of the most prestigious streets in the New Town. Boasting many famous residents in the past it is now the location of the First Ministers residence, Bute House. It was also once home to an otherworldly piano player and it is to this we now turn. The following incident recorded by the Edinburgh Psychic College took place circa 1947, after an intriguing letter was delivered to their HQ in Fettes Row. Consisting of first-hand statements from two tenants on the square, it detailed what occurred during their tenancy. The flat on the upper floor had appeared normal at first but within a short while both tenants reported hearing footsteps on the stairs. They were often heard approaching their flat, but on investigation nothing was found. Perhaps it was just an echo from below they surmised, after all the communal was often quite noisy. One afternoon, on hearing the same steps approaching, the witness was alarmed to hear they had entered the flat. The occupant, now in a state of fear, listened as they entered the drawing room, before the sound of someone playing the piano started up. The sound was so exquisite that the young woman listened at the door for some minutes, before curiosity got the better of her. Entering in the hope of being introduced to her flatmates talented companion, she found nothing but an empty room. Her friend returning sometime later oblivious to proceedings, was taken aback at the news. The subsequent research that was undertaken then revealed the flat in which they were staying had once belonged to a seminary for young ladies. And at the top, once sat the music room. Today, I assume the building is still lived in, but whether the piano playing continues, I cannot say.

Speaking off the New Town and music, this intriguing addition was taken from an interview conducted by 'The Times' some years ago. The subject of the article was musician Paul Haig, former front man of Edinburgh band Josef K, and in it the readers were treated to some anecdotes one of which concerned a haunting. I of course was intrigued, however he omitted to disclose the exact location. Soon after moving, he was treated to some rather spectacular incidents, which included the television coming on by itself. Stranger yet was the sight of the attic hatch having been pushed upwards from below and placed on its side during the night. He of course, being the sole occupant, had observed it being firmly shut on retiring the previous evening. The ceilings in many New Town flats are extraordinarily high, and having lived in one such property, I can vouch that a ladder is generally needed to reach the ceiling. So, what had lifted the hatch? There was no rational explanation. His girlfriend at the time then proposed a visit to a local spiritualist church and so with an open mind they went along. During the evening his curiosity was rewarded by the medium who went onto explain his uncle was present and that he wanted to impart a message. It provided little comfort to find that the main thrust of his 'message' concerned his flat. Rounding off the article the musician then described seeing an apparition within the property, stating: 'the most frightening thing that ever happened was when my girlfriend got up from bed and I noticed a hazy presence follow her out of the room. I thought I was the only person to see it, but when she came back in, she said, "yeah something just walked out of the door behind me," as casual as you like. I couldn't sleep for hours.' He continued to stay in the property for some years and if anything, further happened I am afraid I cannot tell.

Though our next tale is of a certain vintage, the clarity in which it is written makes me believe it to be genuine. The lady in question had nothing to gain from its airing other than incur derision so one must assume it was for her peace of mind. The story featured in a 1942 edition of The Scotsman caused quite a stir at the time and recounts a haunting that took place some sixty years prior in 1878. The location was Meadow Place and concerned her grandmother and two aunts, referred to in the article as the tenants. In the article it described how the tenants received a visit from an old friend, Mrs. Cowan. Before heading home, she went to the upstairs bedroom to collect her hat and coat which had been placed there on her arrival. On preparing to leave she had a strange encounter which prompted her to return to the front room. The ladies still taking tea, were surprised as she enquired who the oddly dressed man was on the staircase? The ladies then stated there was no such man, but Mrs. Cowan insisted that she had just passed him. She then went on to describe the incident in detail and stated that on leaving the bedroom she had encountered the man on the bend of the stairs. Being an obvious gentleman, he had stood back to let her pass. What piqued her curiosity though was his eccentric attire. She described him as wearing tussore trousers with a matching coat and a gaily coloured turban and sash which he wore around his waist. He muttered something to her on passing which she took to be Hindustani. The ladies were at a loss and Mrs. Cowan now equally puzzled left for home. Not long after their youngest uncle, returning from South America paid a visit. The gentleman in question was aged twenty and was roomed on the first-floor bedroom. At breakfast the next day he was quoted as saying, 'why were you girls kicking up such a row in the attic over my head, around 2 o' clock.' The puzzled girls naturally questioned the validity of his accusation. He was however adamant and went on to say that he heard dragging furniture and a chest of drawers being opened then slammed. To cap it all the sound of what he took to be a pistol shot then followed. The girls denied all, and their conversation was put on the back burner. Sometime later the grandmother then made some tentative enquiries to the landlord as regards his previous tenants who reticently explained the following. He explained that prior to their moving in a very eccentric man had lived there. He was an ex-military man and habitually wore Indian fashion having served abroad. One night for reasons known only to himself he entered the attic, barricaded the door and took his own life using a pistol. The letter ended abruptly with no further explanation. Whether the house stands today we can only guess given the address was omitted, however as a potentially true ghost story it takes some beating.

Next up, and to prove this is a cultured tome we take a quick foray into the Modern Art Gallery situated near the Ravelston area of the city. It is a building I have visited many times over the years though it never occurred to me that it might potentially be haunted; therefore, I was delighted to receive the following account from an old friend, artist Catriona Platten. Though only a one-off experience it has left me intrigued and so in due course I hope to find out more. The building, once a school is a labyrinth of corridors and rooms, or so it has been described, the public areas being only the tip of the iceberg. Tasked with setting up the café before opening time she recalled being there at around eight in the morning. This what she said: 'I was working in the café, putting out chairs and setting up. I stopped in my tracks when I saw at the end of the room what I thought was an old man sitting hunched over a table. I was annoyed at first as we didn't open till 9.30 and I turned away muttering under my breath. I then turned back, and he was gone. I searched around but could not find him. I will never forget it; it was like looking at a photograph rather than a real person.'

Moving onto the Grassmarket which is reputedly rife with spiritual activity notwithstanding the impressive choice of pubs therein. The areas name derives from the feed that was once spread across its stones from which the cattle ate having been driven through the aptly named Cowgate. This sprawling market existed for over 500 years until 1919 when the last livestock markets took place. Today's market, a sort of nod to the past is more genteel, selling crafts, street food and vinyl. Historically the area was also synonymous with poverty and the overcrowding even worse than in the closes of the High Street. Although hard to believe the residents of the High Street took great delight in their imagined superiority, referring to those in the Grassmarket as, 'the worms of the earth.' If ever there was a case of 'fur coat and no knickers', then this was it! By the early 1800s, many Irish immigrants had now settled in the area and the overcrowding described as being 'almost unimaginable,' was rife. Descriptions of finding twenty-four people crammed into a double bedroom were not uncommon and a proliferation of ale houses and brothels only added to its reputation. It was a playground for the near destitute, who frittered away what little they had to escape the drudgery. In 1828, locals also ran the risk of finding themselves atop the anatomists table courtesy of Messrs. William Hare and William Burke. Possibly the world's first recognised serial killers, they resided in nearby Tanners Close where they plied their evil trade providing specimens for the anatomists. Being partial to drink and a bit of gambling which they could ill afford they hatched a plan. Being the age of discovery, those in the field of medicine were making great advances, however at the nearby University, there was a dire shortage of fresh cadavers. Resident there was the surgeon Robert Knox, a gifted but flawed human being who was none too picky about how his subjects were procured. Who they were when alive was of little consequence and if the specimens were fresh, he would it was said, pay around seven pounds and ten shillings. A great incentive indeed. Dr Knox who also enjoyed a good lifestyle from his efforts was popular with students, but as is often the case greed was his downfall.

And so, for around ten months in the year 1828 the enterprising pair, who thought of themselves as businessmen literally made a killing but being uneducated and base in their needs they remained in poverty. Now picking up the waifs and strays of the city they would ply their victims with drink till they were inebriated before suffocating them. Even today there is much debate as to how many fell afoul of the pair. Thinking themselves untouchable they made a series of sloppy mistakes including killing locals and within a short time were apprehended. 16 charges of murder were eventually brought against them though some suggest that figure is conservative. Now languishing in Calton gaol the four defendants, Burke, Hare and their partners began the blame game, each proclaiming their innocence. In frustration the judge offered a pardon to those who told the truth and in a touching testament to their friendship, the three accomplices blamed Burke. Suffice to say the judge, a man of his word, freed the prisoners who narrowly escaped being lynched before literally running out of the history books and what fate befell them is shrouded in mystery. Knox already hiding in London suffered the indignity of being associated with murderers and all things considered got off very lightly. He did however become persona non grata amongst his new colleagues, news travels fast. Burke was then hung in front of a baying mob which some suggest exceeded forty thousand people, before his body was gifted to anatomists. His subsequent dissection then caused much excitement with pushing crowds, frayed tempers and people jostling, much like the Fringe I would imagine. Everyone literally wanted a piece of him and to this end some enterprising students, fashioned several small pocketbooks from his slowly shrinking carcass. But anyway, back to ghosts.

Apart from its dark history, the Grassmarkets roster of haunted venues is impressive, even by Edinburgh's standard. There have been riots, countless hangings, murders and that is just the tip of the iceberg. There are around at least five haunted pubs, three haunted hotels and I daresay numerous haunted homes. In one such flat the residents described how they quite often saw the shadow of what appeared to be a man wearing a tall hat. His favoured spot was a corridor where he was seen to walk down it. The couple witnessed this through a glass panel on the door and being the only two people in the flat were in no rush to investigate. The owner also described how her mother who was visiting, ended up trapped in the bathroom while something held the handle from the outside. I assume it was not her husband. As recently as August 2022 further tales continue to emerge and in one instance, I spoke briefly to a visitor renting an Airbnb near the' Last Drop' pub. She described an experience she had on arrival in the morning in which she was convinced she saw a white human like shape which drifted past her eyeline. During our conversation she asked my opinion on whether I thought the area might be haunted. When I said I believed so she looked a little queasy. Her friend then indicted that neither of them were particularly looking forward to going back to their apartment. As we have already looked at haunted hostelries and hotels in the area, we now move on.

Hospitals, potentially the most haunted of all buildings get scant attention compared to pubs and theatres. People claim the spirits of the deceased would naturally prefer to visit a place where they had fun as opposed to not, which of course makes sense. Having spoken to many nurses and the occasional doctor over the last while, many have admitted having seen things that go beyond the rational. Death bed apparitions are the most common of course with departing souls being witnessed, though in the following it would appear there are still those who prefer to linger. Our first location is the former Beechmount hospital. Built for Sir George and Lady Mary Anderson, the governor of Bank of Scotland, today it is used by Environmental Scotland. The following account told to me by Alison Gardiner-Kidd, involved her aunt Jean McWhirter, who in 1991 worked there as a nurse. Undoubtedly used to strange sights, the nursing staff on her ward had their own resident spirit in the shape of a little black boy. Being seen frequently by many witnesses, especially at the time of a patients passing he was known to have a particular fondness for hanging around the storeroom. Seen on many occasions entering the room ahead of staff his appearances were unsettling. Perhaps it was the toys contained in the storeroom that he was drawn to? Unfortunately, he remained anonymous despite his frequent appearances. Alison went on to say. 'My auntie said, that before she entered the storeroom, she used to throw something in.' A sensible move.

Soon after, Grace Ross also a nurse and self-described sceptic, was kind enough to send me the following which occurred in the late 1980s. I was told that at the time when on nightshift, staff were allowed to use the kitchen. Some however found preparing their snacks a little nerve racking due to the resident cook being a ghost. It was said that he or she was known to have a penchant for bacon and its unmistakable odour would randomly fill the air despite no one using the facilities. Grace takes up the story; 'We alternated where we worked and, on this occasion, I was upstairs. We had all taken our breaks. It was around 4am and the strong smell of frying bacon filled the ward. I went to have a look to see who it was, but the kitchen was in darkness.' She then went on to describe another incident. 'At the end of the ward the double door was kept locked at night and on this occasion, I noticed someone entering the toilet, we checked but everyone was in bed. I saw, who I imagined was Mary.' (Mary was the wife of original owner George Anderson)

She went on to say that on a nearby deep windowsill, sat three ornamental vases and it was a popular place for people to use as a seat. One day while sitting on the sill reading, one of the vases literally sprang from the sill and landed on the floor. It gave her quite a fright and the sister on hearing the noise came out of her office to ask what happened. On seeing the nurses distressed demeanour, she remarked; 'Is that Mary, being up to her old tricks?' It was widely believed among staff that Mary was still present on occasion, but whether she was the phantom cook remains a mystery. Sticking with hospitals, we next turn our attention to the Old Royal Infirmary. Now converted into flats and student accommodation, they look swanky though I suspect potentially haunted if one alludes to their previous incarnation.

This story dates from 2001 and was supplied by a former nurse, named Bindy who on that occasion was stationed on a ward in the medical corridor. This is what occurred that night. 'In the middle of the night I went to take my break and saw a woman with black hair, a bright green Alice band, floral shirt and pair of green flares open the door to the staff toilets and go in. I assumed it was a domestic, but she failed to reappear despite the nurse's station having a clear view.' A subsequent investigation revealed nothing to the startled witnesses. Toilets of course are a popular place for ghost to hang out, or so it would seem, and I have heard of around twenty such sightings. Taking place in community centres, pubs and schools, the accounts uniformly describe, 'people,' using the facilities who fail to reappear.

Not to be left out, The Western General has also had its fair share of unsettling incidents, including the following example, described by an ex-nurse while on night duty. Returning to her station she was surprised to see a patient wearing a very old-fashioned nightgown coming towards her. Nothing unusual you might say, except this was the middle of the night and the patient being elderly did not belong in that area. The nurse stopped to observe and noted there was something distinctly odd about the woman. She continued to stare until the truth dawned. The patients' legs had disappeared through the floor. In shock she could only stare as the woman walked right through her, before vanishing. The nurse was traumatised by the experience. I read some time ago of a similar incident when a witness described the ghostly figure of an old woman only being seen from the waist upwards. A bizarre spectacle indeed and possibly quite terrifying. This however gives credence to the argument that many ghosts are mere 'recordings from the past,' as the level of the floors in that building had changed due to an earlier fire. Perhaps this had been the case in the hospital, or possibly the shade had been connected to a much earlier building? With so much death associated with such building's stories are plentiful, and their abundance would fill a book alone, so for now let's move on.

The ghost story collector, of course hopes for nothing more than a juicy morsel, which will, they hope, prove the existence of life after death or in the worst case just provide a good tale. Edinburgh has many, literally hundreds, and a quick trawl will invariably throw up some lesser stories and small anecdotes. Recently, I read for example that in Muirhouse Gardens a local paper reported that the area was said to be haunted by an evil looking man with wild looking eyes and long matted hair. Nothing more was said and to fair the description could match any number of the 'characters' who frequent the town.

Nearby Granton harbour and the nearby Wardie steps have also come under the spotlight for being potentially haunted. Built in 1896 to connect Lower Granton to Granton Road, the steps are allegedly haunted by a faceless entity. Witnessed by residents and the occasional unlucky passer-by the stories follow a familiar theme with the figure motionlessly watching those who come across it. It is known that some have had genuinely frightening experiences. To add further to the mystery a man dressed like a cavalier has also been seen in the vicinity nearby the Royal Yacht Club but as their descriptions vary, we can assume they are unconnected.

And now something a little more disturbing as a short walk along the shore, now brings us to Leith and Graham Street where in 1971, Rob Harrap, along with his partner Patricia and a mutual friend rented a basement flat. The building was described as five stories high and a beautiful example of Georgian architecture, of which the city is famous. Rob told me that his landlady Dora Noyce, who he assumed knew nothing of its history, perhaps unwittingly allowed them to move in. On entry, the tenants felt blessed with the arrangement however the couple's relationship happy at first, quickly soured. Blamed on the oppressive atmosphere within the property, he described something unidentifiable, a presence, potentially malignant, which created an almost tangible sense of brooding menace. Their friend then wisely voted with his feet a short time later.

Despite this, the couple persevered, but soon after they were plagued by a series of unexplained events when personal items began to vanish. For instance, one morning, Rob found his laces unaccountably missing from his shoes. Afterwards something began to loosen his guitar strings during the night. Weeks passed and the sense of unease heightened, only relieved on leaving the flat. The final straw, unexpectantly came soon after, on returning from a night out, when on entering, they were forced to flee by an indescribable sensation of dread within the property. They hurriedly left though to this day Rob remains convinced that something tried to drag him back into the flat. They then endured a four-mile walk before finding a haven for the night. Unfortunately, the couple split up soon after. Sometime later, Rob in a last gesture of goodwill, then volunteered to retrieve the goods that were still inside the flat. Convinced there was a malignancy within the property he brought along a friend on that occasion. On entering he quickly discovered that a large knife usually found at the sink, was now embedded at head height on the reverse side of the door and remains convinced it was thrown by the entity. At the end of his communication, he told me that at that time he was the only key-holder. After that he never went back and for many years pondered over the cause of the disturbance, until the properties eventual demolition. The subsequent discovery of human remains, found directly below the basement, only added to the mystery. Who they belonged to is unclear however, he believes this to be the source of the haunting.

Another obscure tale and one that has more in common with good old-fashioned hysteria rather than the supernatural, is that of Auld Reekie's very own 'Spring-Heeled Jack.' Just what the legendary terror of old London town was doing north of the border is a matter for conjecture? Described as being able to leap entire buildings in a single bound 'Spring-Heeled Jack' was the product of a lurid fantasy, straight out of the pages of a Penny Dreadful, a character who along with 'Varney the Vampire' embodied the Victorian preoccupation with spookiness and morbidity. Accompanying illustrations portrayed a demonic looking moustachioed dandy, which as you will see makes Edinburgh's counterpart a little underwhelming. Patently a much tardier dresser he was described during his fifteen minutes of fame as being dressed all in white with a phosphorescent glow to his face, potentially reminiscent of Alec Guinness's, 'Jacob Marley.' Uncertain where he would strike next and more importantly what his motivations were, he appeared to take great delight in frightening those he accosted. Woman, children and grown men all fell victim, and his uncanny knack of jumping out at passers-by, unaware of his presence, made him akin to todays 'Jumper ooters'. He certainly didn't leap tall buildings in a single bound as did his London namesake.

The first victim, a respectable business owner situated in Princes Street was taken by surprise near Fountainbridge while traversing a quiet road, by the sight of a white clad figure which sprang upon him. In shock, the alarmed businessman then raised his cane in defence resulting in his attacker leaping, 'twelve yards down the road,' before disappearing round a corner. A second appearance was soon reported and this time the victim was a young boy. Rescued by a local resident, the terrified lad blurted out his story describing a figure also dressed in white who suddenly sprang upon him from a nearby street. His rescuer, a kindly lady, then sheltered the poor mite till the law arrived. A further attack followed in quick succession this time in Leith, the victims being two young women. Described in a local paper as walking to their work near the high school. On reaching Leith links the pair were shocked by the sudden appearance of a white clad 'apparition,' resulting in one fainting while the other fled. Afterwards there were no further reports and as short lived as it was, it probably had the desired effect giving him a couple of good newspaper headlines to gloat over. Being 'Spring Heeled Jack' takes commitment and the attacks were undoubtedly the result of human agency rather than anything supernatural. And the miscreant whatever his motivation, we assume got bored.

And now a mystery location in which the witness only describes the area as having offices on the edge of an industrial estate that were converted from a WW2 military hospital. The nearby houses, we are informed, was typical 1960s council stock. The provider of the tale, written under a pseudonym posted this offering on a paranormal forum, asking if any contributors had heard of a similar tale. In due course one person said they had but in a moment of selfishness neglected to post a response. The thread, like an un-watered plant then unfortunately died leaving the following in isolation. Undoubtedly a disturbing experience it was written with enough conviction to suggest that the author was equally perplexed. In his post he went on to describe that it was wintertime and with the weather turning it was bleak, though despite this at lunchtime he would occasionally go for a walk. In the nearby estate there were several food outlets, and barbers, and it was on a visit to the latter that the incident occurred. After getting his haircut he retraced his steps, but on glancing to the right he noticed a little boy. He assumed he was pre-school age by his height and was standing on the opposite side of the road. He stated the boy would have been around the distance of five or six cars down from where he stood. It was then he double-took and noticed with a sickening jolt that the boy's face contained no features, neither eye, nose nor mouth. He stated, 'his face was just hollow skin, and it was if his head had been sucked in from the back, looking like a hole poked into dough.' The boy remained standing for a moment more before turning and disappearing, leaving him in a state of mild shock. Unsure of what he had witnessed it took some moments to come to his senses, before briskly walking back to the office. Sometime later, subsequent walks in the same area yielded no further clues. He said afterwards, that although he had occasionally gone back to the same spot, he always hoped not to see him. He further described that it was an 'intense,' experience and felt 'wrong.' Several comments then appeared in the forum, but no further clues were identified. Perhaps it had been the scene of a tragedy at some point or perhaps an accident had occurred there, someone suggested? It may have even been something far worse.

Another creepy tale, this time associated with a contemporary crime, has intrigued locals for many years and concerns the post-mortem appearances of a murder victim. Whether it's a genuine case of the supernatural remains open to speculation, but here are the facts. In 1996 a resident of Leith, described as being an eccentric character became known locally as the 'cat man of Ferry Road.' His real name was Gilbert O' Donnell and earned his sobriquet from habitually feeding cats. It was not uncommon to see him putting out saucers of milk for neighbouring strays and was also known to feed pigeons and other birds, sometimes carrying bags of crumbs as he walked around Leith. Described as a loner and deemed harmless he nevertheless attracted the ire of those who saw his hobby as attracting vermin. I first became aware of the unfortunate chain of events through a friend and my subsequent research revealed various newspaper articles on the case. In brief, Mr. O' Donnell, was murdered by a neighbour which eventually led to a conviction. However, in a bizarre twist at least three witnesses allegedly saw the deceased after the time of his death going about his business. This resulted in the guilty party's appeal against the charges who argued, how he could have killed him, if the victim had still been alive?

The transcript of the appellants subsequent appeal which took place March 1999 two years after his guilty verdict, is I assume, as close to the truth as one can get and therefore have used it as the basis of this story. On Saturday March 2nd at around 1.45am, a long running feud between O' Donnell and his upstairs neighbour erupted into violence. The perpetrator had been drinking and, on his return, had words with the deceased. Raised voices were heard, a scuffle broke out, followed by a series of loud thuds and crashes. On questioning, the tenants in the block provided witness statements some claiming to have heard nothing while others lay awake, no doubt fearful of what was taking place. Either way no one investigated.

On Sunday March 3rd, the police were eventually summoned by a concerned neighbour. As the story unfolded it was found that on the night of the attack the victim had on his possession a hammer, which according to the account, he had attempted to strike his neighbour. The blow though inflicting an injury merely enraged his attacker and in a blind rage a sustained assault took place, which I will not dwell on. The victim, it was discovered later, would have been dead within minutes of the attack. On the discovery of his body the police then began the process of interviewing neighbours and locals to piece together his last hours.

In the transcript of his appeal, the attacker was described as then visiting a local doctor's surgery on the Saturday morning, where it was noted, he appeared to have scratches on his neck and a head wound consistent with blunt force trauma. While waiting to be seen he intimated to the receptionist, that he was surprised his neighbour wasn't "over here today, because he would be pretty sore." His arrest soon followed, and it was then things got stranger as during the initial trial, four witnesses swore under oath, to have seen O' Donnell very much alive after his alleged murder. The following post-mortem only added to the mystery, describing his death occurring in the early hours of Sunday.

As mentioned earlier, in a bid to have his sentence quashed there then followed a second hearing. Under cross examination, witness number one, Isabella Stewart stated she saw the deceased walking down Ferry Road carrying two carrier bags and wearing a dark jacket and white jeans which was his normal attire. It was around 5.30 on Saturday morning, which she remembered clearly as she had to take her daughters dog out for a walk at that time. The deceased was then observed making his way to the nearby library where he began feeding the pigeons. She had witnessed this on many occasions, and it was a familiar sight. At one point she clearly remembered that he leant forward to pick up some dropped bread and she noted he appeared to be stiff in his movements. Could she have been mistaken, she was asked under oath? But she was adamant and being just around fifteen feet away, she had quietly observed him for some minutes before returning home. She further went on to state that he looked ill, as though he had a bad night's sleep. The police however remained unconvinced, perhaps she had mixed up the dates, suggesting that perhaps she had seen him on the Friday? Isabella sticking to her story then produced a diary in which she recorded various appointments and in it the entry described her daughter's unexpected illness resulting in the early morning dog walk. This was followed by an entry describing an appointment with the local surgery in which she had picked up her daughters' prescription. This was then corroborated by the doctor. Then came witness two, who was ideally placed being the deceased's upstairs neighbour. Sandwiched between the protagonists flats she claimed to have seen him at 9.30 am returning from a local shop. In her statement, she witnessed him enter the building ahead of her and once inside she could plainly hear the bag he carried, bouncing against the railings. She then witnessed him standing at his door but not entering which at the time she found odd. On passing he did not look at her nor acknowledge her, even though he usually said hello. Under questioning, she stated that he had looked pale and white. The 3rd and 4th witnesses, both workers at a newsagent in Great Junction Street further added to the confusion by claiming he had also visited their shop on Sunday. Being a regular and with an unmistakable appearance, he was on this occasion served by both the witness and her assistant, Steven Robbins. Steven was thirteen at the time and was the Sunday help. On O' Donnell's visit, he was thought to have purchased bacon and bread. Similar items were then found mere hours later sitting in his hallway, which begs the question, were they the same purchases or had Steven been called in on the Saturday instead, and simply forgot? The case itself took around a year to reach the courts so perhaps memories were a little vague and the shop assistant they argued, seemed a little confused during questioning.

The defence then suggested that the victim suffered two beatings, a lesser one and a fatal one, and that the accused was guilty of the first while a second assailant finished the job. This was thrown out quickly and a guilty verdict reached despite the inconsistencies of witness statements. A trial of course deals in facts and the idea of a ghost being involved in the proceedings was never brought into play. Some argued that the injured man, merely went about his business, passing away later due to his injuries, a theory quickly refuted by the pathologist's report which stated, that it would have been impossible for him to have even made it down his stairs as death occurred within minutes of the attack. It remains a mystery to this day, and as far as I am aware there have been no further incidents. Perhaps it was a type of crisis apparition all be it a little out of sync, perhaps it was all down to human error?

On a final note, and speaking of the latter, I was told of a similar incident around thirty years ago. At the time my friend's mother was expecting a grocery delivery from her local shop. She lived in a small town and back then a young lad on a grocer's bike did the deliveries. It was a quiet place and most folk kept their doors unlocked so the delivery boy could let himself in. On this occasion my pal's mother was distracted due to cleaning and though aware of the boy coming into the kitchen, indicated he should leave the provisions on the table. She of course had acknowledged him, but on receiving no answer glanced up to find he had gone. On closer examination she found nothing had been left on the table, yet she was convinced she had heard him place them there. Soon after she phoned the shop only to hear terrible news, the lad had been killed that morning while on his rounds. It had been the result of a reckless driver. And that is a true story.

And now, in keeping with tradition, I have saved the best till last. This truly chilling tale took place in 1997 in Lansdowne Crescent in the city's West End. The unwitting householder, my old neighbour David B, kindly discussed the details of what happened which I will relate now. Having bought the flat on the top floor of an elegant Georgian Street, he found by looking at the deeds that its previous owner was the 'Bishop' of St. Marys Episcopal Cathedral on nearby Palmerston Place. Anyone familiar with the Haymarket area of the city will recognise the building which dominates the skyline of the west end. David keen to put his stamp on the property then began the arduous task of upgrading. It had been, he surmised, a rented property for many years and the presence of coin meters suggesting thus. Perhaps it had been rented to students? The ensuing renovations included reinstalling open fires, replastering walls and insulating the roof areas, all of which took time and effort. lastly the flat was painted completely. Sometime later the first stirrings occurred, and a heavy atmosphere descended upon the property. Speaking to David recently he intimated that perhaps the renovations had been the catalyst?

Uneasiness of course could be put down to anything, and at first the odd feelings were almost insignificant however that changed on what he described later as the 'first night.' On that night he recounted waking with a feeling of dread and was shocked to see a figure in the room, floating above his bed. Lying transfixed and unable to move, he could only stare. On being asked what the figure wore, he answered a cassock, and the figure was smiling, 'but it was not a nice smile.' The man then vanished before his terrified eyes. We can only imagine the discussions that followed, however his partner seemed impervious to the situation and remained so throughout. David was not so lucky and sometime later a second incident occurred. As before it took place in the middle of the night only this time, he awoke to find himself physically pinned down by the shoulders. He described it as a terrifying experience yet whatever was responsible remained unseen. Afterwards he routinely slept in the second bedroom and allowed his pet dog to sleep with him, his nerves now rattled from the previous encounters. A further period of calm then followed until one morning, while in the bath, he was aware of a sharp stinging sensation. Painful enough to warrant investigation, he noticed in the mirror a series of long scratches down his back. He had no recollection of how they got there but he imagined the worst.

In a bizarre turn of events, he was then disturbed by two further encounters the first while leaving the flat one morning. In this instance his attention was drawn to a strange looking woman loitering near the steps to the property, who on his approach stepped in front of him. Somewhat taken aback she stood blocking his way before fixing him with, 'a long hard stare.' He described the experience as unnerving and after her curiosity appeared satisfied, she turned wordlessly and walked away. He described her as being her mid-thirties with long hair. He then stated, 'the first thing I thought of when she stood there was, witch.'

On a separate, but equally baffling occasion, David was alerted by the buzzer and on pressing the entry button stepped onto the landing to see who had entered. It was a policeman who on noticing him, stopped half-way up and fixed him with a very uncompromising stare. David somewhat anxious by the policeman's demeanour called down asking if he could be of assistance, and the man like the woman before, turned wordlessly and left. He stated that he felt both incidents were somehow connected. Had a previous owner made enemies? Were these people looking for someone, or worse still had they mistaken him for that person? It was hugely disconcerting, and those questions haunted him for weeks afterwards. To be accosted by two random people was highly unusual particularly as they displayed such naked aggression and his despair wondered if the 'policeman,' had been one at all. Fantastical as it might seem, he began to consider that the previous occupants had quite possibly dabbled in the occult.

The idea of the flat having been used for some diabolical ceremony was not unfounded as soon after an even more terrifying occurrence took place. Around the same time as before, he awoke with a shout, witnessing a half-formed figure in the gloom. He then described to me what he saw, and in this instance, I will let his own words suffice, 'I know this sounds strange but the only way I can describe it was like a giant shrimp, with these legs kicking out in all directions. It felt dark, demonic.' A sleepless night then followed, one in which the lights were kept on. Convinced, that whatever it was had targeted him, he looked for answers but there was none. Typically, his relationship began to disintegrate and ended soon after.

Sometime later when the flat had sold, he told me, he returned for one last look. On entering, he heard a distinct sharp intake of breath. He did not tarry. Coincidentally, in the aftermath of the sale he had the opportunity to talk with the new owner, and in doing so tactfully enquired, if they had any issues concerning the property? They seemed perfectly happy, and thankfully the subject of ghosts never cropped up. To this day, David is convinced that the entity had specifically targeted him. But for what purpose? He also still wonders, if there was any connection between the previous owner, the church and the ghostly priest? On finishing our conversation, I concluded that I have no desire to visit that particular property, even if given the chance.

Ghosts of the Royal Mile

The Royal Mile as you would expect is rife with dark tales of witchcraft, ghosts and cannibalism, some of which I have already mentioned. But there always room for some more, so for now we will look at the following which have taken place in this most venerable of streets. The Lawnmarket, situated at the top end and near the Witchery is our first stop and the incident was recalled by Laura, 'I stay near the top of the Royal Mile in a tenement dated 1886. From time to time, I've suddenly felt a strong sensation of someone close behind me. It only happens occasionally and there is no pattern to it, but it is undeniably there. The previous owner of the flat had commented on it, before I moved in. I thought it was just a silly story until I encountered it one night while playing bass through my headphones. It was so strong I jumped up thinking someone had broken in, but there was nothing to be seen. Since then, it's come and gone and I've gotten used to it, there no malevolence just a strong presence.'

Taking place in relatively modern times, 1977 to be precise, a series of frightening encounters were enough to convince staff at a Lothian Council building, that it was haunted. Such was the belief in what was taking place, that a council spokesman was asked for a quote by a local newspaper. This is what he said 'we are carrying out an investigation. It is an old building, and we are forever getting reports of noises and sightings.' The building situated on St. Giles Street lies almost opposite its namesake, the cathedral, and today is home to a courthouse and some restaurants. Described as a city centre office block, the witnesses were naturally cleaners, who in my opinion, should get danger money. It is true to say that most sightings take place in quieter times, and when better than in the early hours of the morning or later in the evening. It is the cleaner's lot, and an ability to cope with the supernatural should be added to job description for anyone applying as a matter of courtesy. Susan, who had literally started a few days prior to the sighting was then interviewed. She said, 'I had only been here for a week. I was in the basement, which is fully lit, but there is a musty feeling down there. I was with another girl called Jeanette when the shape appeared. It was a grey mass with two blinking white eyes. I turned and looked at Jeanette. We just stared at each other and ran as fast as we could, leaving the vacuum cleaner on.' Afterwards their co-worker Sheila, on hearing the commotion and noticing how scared they were, accompanied them back downstairs where the vacuum was found to still be running. Sheila said afterwards, 'I have never seen the ghost, but I can feel its presence. I call it Horace, and chat to it.' The council premises were rumoured to have been built upon the site of an old stables, and the spirit was thought to be that of a stable lad. Why staff came to this conclusion is anyone's guess, but the sightings allegedly continued.

Retracing our steps to nearby Stevenslaw court and its environs, we look at a historic or perhaps hysteric haunting. You decide. In 1827 the Edinburgh Weekly Chronicle published the details of an allegedly true ghost story which took place on the High Street. The headline read; 'A true and particular account of the disastrous circumstances attending the horrible and most awful appearance of a ghost which took place in a house in the High Street of Edinburgh on Wednesday evening 17th October 1827.' The article went on to say that; 'we have heard of brownies, ghosts, hobgoblins, having caused a great deal of trouble to the human race in various parts of the world, particularly in earlier times. Though some are said to be very useful and done considerable service, they are evidently decreasing in number; in latter times or returning to more favoured parts of the world.' With an opening salvo like that, it is no wonder the subject of ghosts, shifted copy. Both quaint and fascinating, the editor alludes to the superstitions of old yet suggests the modern ghost may have taken a sabbatical. Maybe there were more luxurious surroundings to haunt, after all the High Street was still on its uppers. The Chronicle then went on to describe the incident to which a startled crowd of five hundred onlookers were drawn. According to the report the assembly was so awe struck in terror they remained silent, as the ghost re-appeared at the window of one of the buildings. Witnessed by multiple people at the time, it was described as dressed completely in white and carried a single candle. It was also noted that it possessed a shadow. That part of the story then concludes with no further detail. Afterwards I began to wonder what became of the crowds. Also, and more importantly, what happened to the ghost, did it just vanish, or did it blow out the candle? We will never know. Perhaps, and I am sure this has crossed a few minds, it was just someone innocently heading off to bed. If that were the case, then I propose the crowd would surely have broken the world record for the single biggest mass gathering of peeping toms in history. I remained unconvinced. Still, with a second appearance now being discussed and putting my cynicism to the side, I read on. Occurring mere days later at nearby 160 High Street, the occupants began complaining of hearing, 'dreadful noises.' Soon the wagging tongues of nearby idlers began to attract unwanted publicity. Passers-by whispered suspiciously, hoping to catch a glimpse of whatever lurked there. They didn't have to wait long, for mere days later, the servants became unwitting media stars while alone in the house.

According to their testimony, the drama unfolded after their employees had left earlier in the evening. Without warning they were horrified to witness a similarly clad, tall gaunt figure now standing in a room off the kitchen. Their wild shrieks now joining the agonised cries of the apparition quickly drew a crowd. Described as sounding like someone in agony, the spirits terrifying demeanour sent them flying for their lives, literally bursting into their neighbour's property to escape. The occupant, a solicitor, described as a respectable citizen was so alarmed at the intrusion that he hid beneath his bed clothes. As was noted their ensuing cries had brought the local populace scuttling like rats from the nearby closes and the crowd now swollen to many hundreds, jostled to get a glance at the ensuing drama. Amid the confusion enterprising members of the public had now arrived pulling a portable fire engine, the assumption being the property was ablaze. Others convinced of the same then began emptying household furniture into the street in lieu of its imminent destruction. It took some considerable time for the police to restore order. The mob, reluctant to return home no doubt grumbled at being denied their fun. The servants, I can thankfully report were given shelter for the night from a kind-hearted neighbour who owned the coffee house below. The populace perhaps uneasy, waited with bated breath for what was to come next, but nothing ever did, at least on that occasion. The police aware of the uneasy mood, and in a rare moment of public relations, allowed, 'three stout hearted policemen,' to hold a vigil in the property the next evening. Any hope of seeing the dreadful apparition for themselves came to no avail as it was never seen again, or if it was no one bothered to record it. The broadsheet concluded by stating, 'they regretted to learn that the health of the girl witness had been seriously affected by fright.' Reading this today we are left with more questions than answers. The descriptions though unintentionally amusing are also unsatisfying, omitting large swathes of information, leaving us to suspect it was a case of mass hysteria.

Before we more on, nearby lies another potential location. This 'encounter,' not regarded as a full-blown haunting still merits inclusion and took place in Paisley Close or 'Heave awa' Close,' if you prefer. Locals will know the story well, but for those who don't it was the location of the last great tenement collapse in the city. In 1861, the venerable building already many hundreds of years old suddenly gave way and collapsed in its entirety, burying around seventy occupants within the rubble. A frantic mob then descended pulling desperately at the mountainous pile. Miraculously there were survivors, the best known being young Joseph McIvor. Pulled from the rubble with nary a scratch upon him, today his beautifully carved effigy sits at the entrance to the close with these immortal words carved beneath, 'heave awa lads I'm no deid yet.' These being the words he allegedly shouted on that fateful day. The close today, houses a recording studio and rented property and it is to one of those we look. Covered by the Evening News in 1983, this small vignette suggests perhaps its gloomy past has left a residue. The property at four Paisley Close was at that time rented by two students from

Napier College who described themselves as being level-headed and not prone to fancy. It was in the month of January that the first occurrence took place when one of the lads distinctly heard his name being called directly into his ear. This of course caused quite a stir. Sometime later and on returning from college a second encounter took place. This is what was said. 'I was walking down the close when I heard footsteps behind me. I continued down and then stopped to look and see who was there but there was no one. I then entered the stair and started to climb, when I heard the footsteps again. I stopped on the stair and looked around, there was no one behind me but the footsteps continued and came right up to me.' He then rushed inside. Afterwards no other incidents of this nature were reported however I did hear someone mention quite recently that workers at the recording studio had suggested it was haunted. Perhaps one day more will come to light.

Further down we now find ourselves, next to the Scottish Parliament building, where a gruesome series of events took place in 1707. Part of the folklore of the Royal Mile, the following has been described as a true story though it is not without its detractors. The location sits next door to the parliament building and is now part of the complex, called Queensberry House. A former 52-room townhouse it had multiple uses including a soup kitchen, military barracks and hospital. Bought by the 1st Duke of Queensberry in 1689 and subsequently inherited by his son the 2nd Duke of Queensberry. He is infamous for supporting the 'Act of Union' between Scotland and England, creating a United Kingdom. The loss of a Scottish parliament was the result. He was not a popular chap.

Of course, for lovers of the macabre this location is best known as the home of an alleged 'cannibalistic idiot.' The cannibal in question was Queensberry's dirty secret, his son James Douglas 3rd Marques. Also known as the Earl of Drumlanrig, he was described as immense in stature and 'an idiot of the most wretched kind, rabid and gluttonous as a wild animal.' Being only ten years of age, he was hidden from the public gaze by a stout door, his life according to accounts being that of a prisoner. As with many gruesome tales it has undoubtedly grown arms and legs over the years, if you pardon the pun. Nevertheless, the aftermath resulted in the family decamping to Leeds, where they lived out there lives away from the gawking citizenry. Perhaps, as one of the main signees of the Treaty of Union, the Duke felt his existence might be somewhat precarious in his hometown? Perhaps it was to avoid further scandal? It's fair to say the story will no doubt have changed in the ensuing years. Today online, it features high on any list of Edinburgh's top ghostly locations, though its veracity has frequently been questioned. Despite this there are those who remain convinced of its supernatural pedigree due to personal experience, and they include obligatory cleaners and former hospital workers.

The origins of the haunting first recorded in 'The Traditions of Edinburgh 1841' states that on the night of the signing, the Marquess along with assorted peers and his entourage enjoyed a convivial and lucrative meeting on the High Street, putting his signature to the document that would change the face of Scottish politics forever. While away, he left house in the hands of a young scullion given the task of preparing their celebratory meal. Avoiding the wrath of the now rioting mobs, he returned hours later than anticipated for the planned feast, but on arrival were met with a curiously silent building. Where were the cries that normally accompanied his child's insatiable appetite? The answer became all too clear as on reaching James's room, they discovered it to be empty and the door ajar. The subsequent search revealed nothing, that is until they entered the kitchen where a curious smell assailed their nostrils. Further investigation revealed a ghastly tableau as the young James was caught in the process of devouring the scullion. According to the story he had broken loose and on discovering the cowering servant roasted him on the very spit, reserved for preparing the feast. If true, one can barely imagine the horror that the poor lad must have felt at the appearance of James Douglas, who undoubtedly cackled with joy at the sight of the terrified boy. The aftermath of the incident, a little cloudy in detail reveals nothing of the scullion's name or indeed where his remains now lie, but the assumption is it was likely in the expansive gardens now a carpark.

The family keen to put a little distance between themselves and the crime then moved within days decamping to Leeds where young James now stripped of his title spent his remaining eight years in an insane asylum. Dying on the 24th of January 1715 at Calverley near Leeds, under the care of a Mr. Richardson. Whether he did commit the deed, or the story was manufactured to discredit an unpopular man, remains open to debate, but we assume his 'mental illness,' was an embarrassment to the family. The mob succinct in their condemnation believed it was God who had punished the family because of the Act of Union. Admittedly not the cheeriest of stories it nevertheless has become ingrained in Edinburgh's grim lore.

Today of course the building at least on the outside looks as it did. Inside changes have taken place and the area is now used as offices and a lounge for MPs doubtlessly only used infrequently due to their herculean labours. So today, the question remains, is it haunted? That I suppose depends on your point of view. Inside, the fireplace where the dark deed allegedly took place still stands and it is there the spirit of a young boy has been seen. Looking forlorn which is an acceptable ghostly demeanour, the figure has been said to vanish on approach. Contemporary accounts of the haunting are I'm afraid, like hens' teeth, however, there have been rumours circulating for years. For example, cleaners working unsociable hours have claimed to have heard the young boys' footsteps echoing on the flagstones and empty corridors of the property. On one occasion the figure of a small boy also witnessed near the fireplace. Though one might argue that a building of such calibre is deserving of a full-blooded haunting, the stories I will admit are a little scant. Things perked up a little though on the discovery of some accounts relating to its time as a hospital.

Appearing in a recent article, the following was described by interviewee Gordon Stewart who is Head of Visitor services at the Scottish Parliament building. Asked during the interview if he had experienced anything supernatural himself, he answered in the negative however he did recount two incidents relating to former occupants. These are his own words: 'The one that really struck home was a couple of years ago, she was the daughter of the governor of the Queensberry House hospital, and the governors house used to stand on Holyrood Road before the parliament. She got in touch to say her family moved out of the house 60 years ago and could she come back and have a look. Her father was the governor, and

I don't think a man given to flights of fancy. She said her father was walking down one of the staircases at Queensberry House which is one that doesn't exist now. At the bottom of the staircase was a little boy who just vanished.' It was also mentioned that when used as a hospital, trolleys and gurneys were described as seen to move by themselves. Gordon then went on to state that more recently in an office on the 3rd floor, it was noted that there was on occasion a very strong smell of roses. It was said to be associated with one of the daughters of the duke who died in a house fire.' Before we move on, a recent article describing the lounge area, indicated that today, MP'S were able to enjoy, possibly the cheapest pints in town. The subsequent outrage expressed by some members of the public in the aftermath of this revelation, was possibly akin to that fateful evening.

Historically, Scotland was regarded of one of the worst places in Northern Europe for its persecution of witches. The King himself, James VI, believed that witches were a real threat, capable of causing great harm and at one point had personally targeted him. Travelling to Copenhagen to meet with future wife Anne, sister of the king of Norway and Denmark, the fleet then ran into a violent storm on their return. During the maelstrom, one ship was lost, and he subsequently came to believe that witches were responsible. A spell had been cast, and the storm was viewed as an assassination attempt. In the aftermath he concluded that Demons being a rod of correction had been sent by God, and witches were their human agency employed to cause mischief. Intrigued by a spate of witch trials from his wife's home country, he was inspired to write, 'Daemonologie.'

Published in 1597 as a three-part essay, it described in detail, the various spirits whose sole intention was to taunt or perhaps tempt man. The book of course is purely a work of fantasy, and within its pages he described what practitioners of the dark arts were capable of. It is still widely available to read, the National Library of Scotland being one source. On perusing the reader will notice a good proportion of the tract deals with the detection and punishment of witches. It's unpalatable and says as much about the man who wrote it and of the mindset of the age. In the book he states that witchcraft was, 'most certainly practiced and that the instrument thereof merits most severely to be punished.' The ensuing madness resulted in the death of around 300 innocent people, mainly women, commencing with the North Berwick Witch Trials. Barbarity of the worst kind then haunted the city for decades thereafter. The public illiterate and gullible were carried along as always, and the accusation of witchcraft proved a great way of ridding oneself of despised family members, neighbours and ministers. The victims, overall being poor, were made up of the lower classes and were picked upon for the flimsiest of reasons. Perhaps someone had heard them talking to themselves? Maybe a farm animal had fallen ill? Perhaps two neighbours had quarrelled, and one was out for revenge? There were many reasons. For the rich and the upper classes there were also noted victims, the accusations now based upon ancient feuds, revenge for perceived wrongs and for political gains. As a guide, I remember initially, including the subject of witchcraft during my tours, however the more I discovered about the barbarity involved the more I wavered in my resolve. It is not a happy subject and one that still needs readdressed by present governments.

Today, they say those dark deeds have left an indelible stain on the Castle Esplanade which is a good way to start any ghostly tale, and in my opinion those deaths literally and figuratively haunt the city to this day. There is one name however which stands out above all others, that of Bald Agnes or Agnes Sampson. Tragically put to death, due to the insanity of a patriarchal society her name has become synonymous with witchcraft. Both a midwife and healer of repute, she was accused of dealing in the black arts. Initially refusing to submit to torture, she was brought before the king at Holyrood Palace. The questioning lasted days and several lurid incidents were recounted, no doubt prompted by her deprivations. The king at first remained unconvinced of her guilt but slowly changed his mind as more evidence was offered. Eventually in the face of overwhelming evidence she was taken to Castlehill and executed. During her trial she suffered the indignity of being shaved, in the belief that the devils mark lay hidden, and thus acquired her unforgettable name. Today her unquiet spirit is said to roam the Palace of Holyrood and though her appearances are infrequent, they are indeed terrifying. Below are two examples.

Taking place in 1990 during a visit by the Chancellor of Germany a young German diplomat was witnessed entering an office to collect some papers. Moments later, a loud shriek was heard to pierce the air and the man was seen to bolt from the room in near collapse. When able to recount what happened, the startled witnesses were horrified to learn, that on entering the room he saw the naked, transparent, floating form of a woman with outstretched arms hovering above the desk. What happened to the diplomat in the aftermath was never noted, though I suspect he had quite a shock. In 2014 an even more disturbing report emerged. On that occasion, a maintenance man repairing a lock, observed the figure of a woman standing at the end of the corridor in which he worked. The woman was described as bald and wearing a white gown of sorts. The figure then slowly began limping towards him, before his enthusiastic screams caused her to vanish. Terrifying.

On a lighter note, four years ago I was in the process of taking one of my first tours and as previously mentioned, I used to include witchcraft. Mentioning the 'deils mark,' I was describing what form this might take including birthmarks, perhaps a blemish or even a third nipple on which a demonic host was thought to suckle. Of course, having a third nipple is, or least I have heard more commonplace than one would assume. On that tour the group numbering around twenty stood on St Giles Street and closest to me stood two women. They were in their early twenties and during the story I then alluded to the third nipple. At that moment I noticed the girl furthest from me mumbling something into her friend's ear before giving her a slight dig in the ribs. The lady turned a dark crimson and on leaning forward plainly hissed the words, 'Fuck off,' to her friend. A mild squabble then erupted before they left the tour abruptly. Afterwards the words pin and drop came to mind. Once out of earshot I assured the group that she must have accused her friend of talking to herself, another sign of being a witch apparently. It was the least I could do.

Heading back up the Royal Mile now, we pass several distinctive closes. One can imagine areas such as these being prey to all manner of strange goings on in the past, and you would be right. They are without a doubt atmospheric and even today can be quite eerie as darkness settles. Speaking of which, I came across the following in a ghost related forum and decided to include it. As with many forums its always difficult to ascertain whether the experiences are genuine but as its quite creepy, I am taking a leap of faith. The location, Chessels court, is best remembered today as the place where Edinburgh man about town and thief, Deacon Brodie, met his fate. Related by a former tenant, who resided there in the 1980s. This is what he wrote: 'One night I had been asleep and got up to get water at around 1.30 in the morning. I climbed back into bed and heard the landlady's dog growling and scratching to get in the door. At that moment something or someone came through the wall by my bed and climbed over me. I felt it pushing down on the blankets. It lasted about two minutes, with the dog all the while growling. It then moved off me, and at that point the dog stopped growling and went back to its bed. I quickly turned the light on. When I explained what had happened, the landlady said she had never heard a thing, claiming that if the dog usually made a noise she would have woken. A downstairs neighbour who had lived in the property below for 40 years visited soon after and he told us how the property looked when he first moved there. He said that the previous owner, an elderly lady, used to have a con-necting door where my bed was now positioned.' Sometime afterwards the landlady's daughter heard of his experience and claimed that she also believed it to be haunted.

Speaking of Chessels court, I read William Bone's 'The Per-ambulator in Edinburgh,' quite recently and was surprised to hear of a similar account. In the book, Bone, suggests Edin-burgh's ghosts of old may have been a combination of the pro-lific 'haar,' (mist) known to billow through Auld Reekie's an-cient closes and entrenched superstition. He then argues that the popular writings of Scott, Chambers, Stevens and Hogg also played their part. Which of course they did. Lastly, he notes that mothers would also use the threat of ghosts to tame unruly children, with one nurse likening them to, 'a man o' haar.' If this was the case, we can only assume the children of Edinburgh must have been particularly well-behaved in the past. The witness a Mrs Gordon, who at the time was living in an ancient house on the lawnmarket, was a former resident of Chessels court. According to her story she bore witness to phenomena on several occasions, though during her discourse remained wonderfully pragmatic. These are her own words: 'I had heard a lot about it, but I never saw it, although I have been near to seeing it. We lived on the top flat and that was where it was said to be, it had been there lang syne. One nicht I was in the room, and I heard somebody breathing hard just outside the door. It was like someone stopping after climbing the stairs before going on. I opened the door and looked out with the candle in my hand. It was naebody-it was the ghost. Mony a time I heard it again breathing hard at the top o' the stairs just as I'm telling you. But I never saw it richt. My guid brother did, O, he saw it and near lost his mind. He was sleepin' in his bed in the big room. It was an old-fashioned room, as maybe you know, with a recess a' carved-like. It must have been a grand room in the auld days. The recess was far too small for him, he being so big, so the bed was sor o' half in the recess and half oot. It was like a tall woman in black silk, and the dress stuck oot a' round an' near took up the hale room, and he couldna see the face o' it, for it had a long black veil covering the hale heid. It was awfu' tall, just as the folk said. Weel, there he was, a' in a sweat and the ghost was clean vanished. He up and on wi' his claes and oot o' the hoose, and that was the last we had o' him, for he wouldna' stop, no' if ye had payed him for it. I had heard say that the women had to do with the recess. She had hanged hersel' or something in the auld times. I never saw her mysel' but I have heard her at the top of the stairs in the dark…breathing hard…just outside the door.' I'm sure you agree her description paints an evocative picture, quite at home in the work of M R James.

Reading on I discovered that unlike Mrs. Gordon, most of the other inhabitants appeared a touch more reticent in discussing old-fashioned notions such as ghosts. Those who did were invariably scorned. It appears though, that Bone remained undaunted and on approaching another elderly citizen in the hope of garnering a further spine-tingler received the following. This time from two neighbours they described the alleged haunting which they had heard from a friend. I quote: 'She was sair troubled with the ghost of a woman in white, moaning and groaning.' On hearing this, her neighbour chipped in. 'I ken what she's efter wi' her ghosts: she wants something ta'en off her rent.' What Bone made of this I'm not sure?

A Fright in the Museum

For our next stop we will visit a few of Edinburgh's renowned museums, most remain open but unfortunately the following has been consigned to the history book. The location of the building was New Assembly Close, near the Tron. Edinburgh Wax Museum was curated by Charles Cameron. An investigator of the paranormal, which he described as 'natural laws,' was well versed in Edinburgh's dark history. The waxworks were one of the city's most popular attractions featuring effigies of all the town's most nefarious characters, not the kind of place you would wish to be locked into. Recounting a brief experience, he had during his tenure he had been crossing the main hall on the top floor of the building to check a door was shut properly. While there his torch sputtered and went out unexpectantly leaving him alone in the pitch black. What happened next sent a chill down his spine as he claimed later that as he stood there, he became aware of children standing around him. They then began whispering to each other. After some frantic moments he managed to get the light back on, illuminating an empty room. Afterwards he described it as a very disconcerting experience, one which he did not care to repeat. The building in case you wondered was formerly used as a children's shelter.

Travelling down the royal mile and incorporated into the Canongate Tolbooth lies the 'Peoples Story Museum,' which as the name suggests is dedicated to the social history of the city. A fabulous museum it is a must see for those interested in the story of the people of Edinburgh and as expected has a few ghost stories to spare. In this regard I spoke recently to a former employee, Kerrie who provided a very insightful story detailing how their school trip was ruined. Here is what happened. 'I worked at the 'People's Story' when I was a teenager and we used to get lots of school groups visiting to learn about Edinburgh. They would make their way around the museum and end up in the projection room, where they would be shown old stories about Edinburgh before leaving. This group of children who were primary school age were coming down the stairs and being hurried out be their guardians. They looked quite upset and the teacher looked annoyed. They approached the desk where my friend and I were standing and told us that it wasn't very funny to be playing jokes at our age. The teacher began to describe seeing a pair of feet dangling from behind the projection screen. We didn't know what she meant. We waited till they had left and started to look around the museum to see if there was anyone causing mischief. We couldn't see anything. We were talking to another member of staff later, who had worked there for many years, and they explained that the projection room was once the area where prisoners were kept on the night before their execution. It is not beyond the realm of possibility that prisoners may have taken their own life. So, we now believe that the children saw an image of a prisoner who was hung behind the screen.'

Having worked in several museums including the Museum of Edinburgh, Kerrie stated, 'one of the worst instances happened in Huntly House or the Museum of Edinburgh. The place holds Greyfriars Bobby's collar and water bowl and we used to hear the dog running about on the wooden floor. Towards the back office of the museum sits what used to be the staffroom and bathroom. In the area there was just a horrible ominous feeling, whatever it was hated us being there and made it obvious. It was full of anger, full of upset and I would not go upstairs on my own. I didn't want to be in there and would take the shortest routes. I would go across to the Peoples Museum just to use their bathroom. If you used the bathroom in the building it would lock you in there, move things and make banging noises. I have no idea what it could have been, but I have not returned since the day I left the job, and I don't think you could pay me enough to go back.'

A short walk up the Royal Mile brings us to my favourite museum in the city, an attraction you will either love or hate, the Museum of Childhood. Allowing the visitor to wallow shamelessly in nostalgia, it is however a Paedophobes nightmare, and their doll collection is both astonishing and terrifying in equal measure. I love old toys but concede some are creepy, none more so than dolls and this museum has them in abundance. Many have argued that perhaps the exhibits themselves are acting like psychic magnets drawing spirit towards them, while the more pragmatic suggest that it's just the sheer volume of antique dolls that are responsible for unsettling visitors. I have visited many times and I must admit that those expressionless eyes can be disconcerting, as are the porcelain brittle faces or those with faint smiles exposing tiny needle-sharp teeth. It's a creepy place. but is it really haunted? I must admit I used to have my doubts having only heard a generic tale or two, including the old classic bricked up children in an orphanage, routine. Today this story has all but been debunked, yet strangely the sound of children's voices is still one of the most reported phenomena. It is a childhood museum of course. Recently I had the good fortune to speak with a couple of witnesses who categorically believe that its haunted, and I imagine when it reopens, I will look at it in a different light. I cannot wait.

Patrick Murray the founder of the museum apparently thought so too, and often recounted feelings of being watched, of hearing strange laughter and whispering coming from empty rooms. Scarily though he claimed also to have heard a child crying, a phenomenon still reported to this day. The current premises, an old Salvation Army Hall has been home to the museum since 1957 and is the oldest in the world dedicated to the subject of childhood. Patrick Murray who passed away many years ago, was well known for his love of toys and his collection formed the basis for the museum, ironically however he was not particularly fond of the very people who might be attracted to it. For example, in a response to a complaint about the gory nature of some of the exhibits, he replied 'Madam this is a museum of childhood, not a museum for children,' which made me laugh.

Heather Burns, whose family have lived on the Royal Mile for generations, contacted me recently regarding her father's experiences. Being a former employee of many keynote attractions, he was well placed to provide some fascinating stories. He was much respected locally and at different times worked in the Tolbooth Museum, Edinburgh Castle and the Museum of Childhood. Here is his story as related to me by Heather. 'My father used to work in the museum and used to go in early with mum. Her job was to clean it. One morning on opening dad smelt something vile, like shit, coming from the staircase where the curator's office was, and went to have a look. He checked the doll's house room and then just has he reached the top floor he heard a lady singing, in not a nice voice. Her ran downstairs immediately grabbed mum, locked up and refused to return. My mum said she had never seen fear in my dad's eyes like it. He refused to speak about it and gave his notice in.' Also of note was the following anecdote which may explain some of the inherent creepiness that people feel in the building. 'The old building was next to a temporary morgue in which I saw dead bodies with my sister, through the windows down the side close of the museum. This was next to McGoos disco (a former Mod club). This was in my lifetime. Dad was shocked when we showed him what we had seen. He immediately contacted the council.'

Another story recently surfaced, lending further weight to the above, this time contributed by Karina Emslie. She described to me that after missing her bus she decided to stay the night at her mums, who lived above the Museum of Childhood, in sheltered housing. Karina stated that on that occasion she woke in the middle of the night to the sound of 'lots of children crying and other weird noises.' What unsettled her most was that there were no children resident, in fact children were not allowed to stay as part of the tenancy agreement. She then went on to say; 'I got up for a drink and looked out of the kitchen window, it looked right into the museums landing 's stairs. It was then that I saw a figure walked past. It was around 3am and the building was in darkness and was shut.' When I asked how she felt, she told me, 'I was freaked out.' Her mum told her afterwards that she believed the building to be haunted.

Lastly, I was passed on this contribution from a former employee, Kerrie. Here is what she told me. 'Another place I worked at was the Museum of Childhood. The building had an eerie feeling about it because of the amount different toys, especially the doll room. Many of the older dolls were made of wax, so the room must be kept at a certain temperature, or they will melt, so even if the temperature is a degree higher when you come in the next day it looks like they have moved. Most of the dolls were donated, and people seemed happy to get rid of them to be honest. Another area that is odd is the one where the staff room was, it used to be an old mortuary where they kept bodies and there's a tunnel that connects the museum with the pharmacy across the road, which used to be a morgue. The room was always freezing, with weird noises being heard and very odd feelings. Opening in the morning or locking up at night always felt strange. While you were sitting doing the float you would always hear things. I refused to go into the back office where the curator used to sit. Like the museum of Edinburgh, the feeling you got was heavy and oppressed, angry and negative, it's a very interesting building.'

Dreading the Boards: Haunted Theatres

Next to pubs theatres it would appear are the next most likely venues to be haunted, and not because of the many performers who have died on stage, ahem. To me there's something intrinsically creepy about a theatre. Whether it's the poorly lit foreboding backstage areas or the cavernous size, they are inherently creepy. I have investigated a few in my time and on one occasion met with a former scenery painter, now archivist, Edi Swan. He likened theatres to a battery storing the energy from the past. If high emotions, good, or bad, are absorbed into the spiritual make-up of a location, then theatres are the perfect spot for some otherworldly activity. The theatre he worked in by the way, was also haunted and Edinburgh's theatres I am pleased to say, do not buck the trend.

Sigmund Berger or The Great Lafayette was born Sigmund Neuberger in Munich 1871 and became the world's highest paid magician, affording him a luxurious lifestyle. Despite this, his wealth and money meant little to him as his main love was animals. He had a particular fondness for dogs and hung a plaque outside his London home which read, 'The more I see of men, the more I love my dog.' His favourite was his

191

much-cherished 'Beauty,' a terrier gifted from fellow illusion-ist Harry Houdini which he doted upon like a child. At night she slept atop velvet pillows, wore diamond encrusted collars and at home had a suite in miniature which included a bath. She also had a strict regime of five meals a day which ironi-cally led to her death, literally putting the die into diet. De-spite this, existing photographs show a dog that is surpris-ingly svelte, so I assume her passing was due to the richness of the diet rather than quantity. Now resident in Edinburgh, and mere four days from commencing his long-anticipated spectacular, the death of his beloved companion was a bitter blow. Despite this he vowed to continue with his tour and so approached Edinburgh council to secure a last resting place for Beauty at Piershill cemetery. They baulked at the sugges-tion; however, Lafayette persuaded them otherwise acknowl-edging the plot would also be his lasting place when his time came. Perhaps after offering a little cash incentive, they agreed. The words proved prophetic however, as soon after he too was to meet his maker. And so as planned on the night of Friday the 9th of May at the Empire Theatre of Varieties', Nicholson Street, Lafayette began his spectacular twenty-five-minute routine the 'Lions Bride.' The audience were capti-vated, the set conjuring images of the orient while a troupe of supporting performers, juggled, danced and contorted. Then a lone female appeared on the stage and entered a cage con-taining a real lion. The mesmerised crowd waited with bated breath until with a mighty roar the beast leapt forward only to reveal Lafayette. Stunned, they rose to their feet clapping. Moments later, according to reports, the upset of a nearby lamp caused the scenery to alight. The sudden conflagration quickly took hold on the stage and only when the fire curtain was lowered did the unsuspecting audience realise it was not part of the act. Mercifully most escaped to safety, Layette included, but returning in a bid to save his horse he perished. Hours later his body along with that of his horse and Lion were found, charred beyond recognition. There were in total ten or eleven casualties depending on which report you read. These included members of the orchestra, stagehands and performers Little Joe and Alice Dale, a tiny fifteen-year-old who worked a mechanical teddy bear. It was an unprecedented tragedy. Some days later in a strange twist another body was recovered in the basement and on closer examination it was found to be the real Lafayette, the previously body, being that of his body double. In the aftermath of the tragedy, there was much outpouring of grief across the world and in Edinburgh his funeral attracted unsurpassed crowds. The sad irony was, both he and beauty could now rest together at Piershill cemetery. The more superstitious, mumbled that his death was the result of a curse brought on by the burial of his beloved dog next to human remains. Nonsense of course, but the strange co-incidence did not go unnoticed. On the day of his interment the funeral procession led by Lafayette's Silver Mercedes slowly wound its way towards his last resting place, its lone passenger being a Dalmatian hound. Of course, from such tragedies do ghost stories spring and since then persistent rumours of his tall dark figure now seen in the current theatre is grist to the mill. Currently known as the Festival Theatre, his sightings are at best sporadic. Perhaps he misses the lights and the applause of his adoring fans? A passing chill, a shadowy figure and seats being raised have all been blamed on Lafayette but of course he is not alone. Others may be equally responsible including the spirit of a peg legged sailor and little girl in a yellow dress, the latter favouring the upper circle. She has been described as having the ability to blow on necks of unwary patrons. Could this apparition be that of Alice Dale? Like pubs, any self-respecting theatre must have ghosts but in the case of the Festival Theatre they remain somewhat elusive.

The next best thing to the shade of a resident actor, must be that of a stagehand and they're plentiful. Take the Playhouse at the top of Leith Walk for example and Albert. This spirit, allegedly a stage door keeper from the past fits the bill nicely. He is thought to have passed away while in the Playhouse, but who he is remains a mystery. Like many other ghosts an affectionate moniker goes a long way to reducing the scare factor, and so he is known as Albert. In the late 1950s, or so it has been rumoured, the police were called to a break in and in classic ghost story tradition, met an old man introducing himself as Albert. He assured the officer there had been no break in and so returning to nearby Gayfield police station, he filed his report. The policeman on returning to the theatre the next day, was of course met by the real stage door attendant, who in tried-and-true fashion, explained that Albert was in fact dead. Cue shocked policeman. How I would love this to be true. It does, as aficionados will recognise have all the tropes associated with a classic ghost story however the fact there have been varying versions raises questions. There are however some worthy contemporary reports and it's to those we now turn. Take for example an article published last year in the Edinburgh News which made for an enjoyable read. In the article various witnesses provided the following meaty anecdotes including one from the then chief technician, Larry McGuire. In his report he stated the following. 'I had gone onto the stage to plug in a wandering lead and saw a figure standing by the cinema screen curtains. The next thing I knew was being helped up from the stage floor by other night staff who had heard me screaming.' Not to be outdone, a second interviewee Keith Donald, recounted this particularly chilling tale, which I quote directly from the article.

'One night I had gone all the way up the North Tower and across the stage, my dog Meg was with me. I was just about to go up the steps of the tower when I realised Meg wasn't with me. I looked back and she was just sitting there staring. I went back and tried to encourage her, but she wouldn't move so I put her on her lead and tried to get her to come out, but she literally went rigid. She looked at me, then to the stair and then back to me as she started moaning and whining. That was enough for me, the South tower didn't get checked that night.'

A second encounter, soon after, proved to be just as creepy, this time taking place in the main foyer. Again, these are his words. 'There are two sets of doors from the foyer to the auditorium and there is a light between them. As I approached the first set of doors, I realised it was dark between them. I went to investigate but as I got closer the light suddenly came on. Chills began to run down my spine as I realised that the darkness which had blocked the light had now moved into the auditorium. The closer I got to it, the further it receded. Terrified by this time I was determined to find out what it was, so I forced myself to go into the auditorium. I couldn't believe what I was seeing. The stage right box was lit as normal, but the stage left one was shrouded at about five per cent of its usual output and I got an awful feeling that someone didn't want me there.'

But before we move on, let's look back to 1997 when the Playhouse Theatre was being used for a Commonwealth government meeting. The security for the event was of course tight, and the police scoured the building in advance using sniffer dogs. At the time nearby theatre staff overheard a conversation between the dog handlers and the chief inspector. It transpired that the building had been given all clear, except level six which the dogs had refused to enter. Staff knew only too well the reason and relayed their story to the police, explaining that this was the favourite hangout for Albert. They took it very well and by all accounts seemed non-plussed. The staff, still left with the predicament of an impending meeting then contacted the castle and soon after the army dog handlers arrived. The team encountered no problems, and the search was completed. Afterwards one staff member asked jokingly if the handlers thought the army dogs were harder than those from the police? They received this straight-faced reply, 'No, but they are based at the castle, so they are used to spooks and spirits.'

My Worst Ghost Tour Ever.

The pitfalls of the ghost tour are manifold. Poor weather is the obvious one, a drenching on the High Street in Mid- December, a chastening experience. But that is the least of it as you will see. 'You have more to fear from the living than the dead,' is oft repeated, and is indeed very true, as you will see. A guide's lot can be an unhappy one, whether its rude guests, drunken passers-by who remark cheerily 'What a load of shite,' or appalling weather it can be a tough gig. Disheartening as this is, there is also the question of recompense and though a successful tour need not be judged solely on the generosity of participants, it helps. Perhaps though the greatest insult to any guide, is the claw. The claw, in case you wondered is the shape a hand makes as it descends upon the guides up turned palm. Usually containing the dregs of a pocket, it will invariably offload a handful of random shrapnel into the unsuspecting recipient's hand. After an hour and a half of emoting this can be somewhat of a let-down for one's efforts and one is left wondering whether the bus home is now a viable option. Pity the guide who is paid in sweeties as they say in Scotland, though literally this has been known to happen. I can attest to this having spoken to recipients of such generous bounties, with one unfortunate colleague, being paid in chocolate. After the gamut of drunks, psychopaths and angry locals has been run, there are still 'your guests,' to consider. Overall, well behaved, at worse a little exuberant the guide rarely needs therapy unless one counts a particularly poorly paid tour. In this instance the guide may question his or her sanity and ask themselves, 'where did it all go wrong?' There are of course distinct types who attend tours, and after a while they are easily spotted amongst the gathering. These include, the eye-rollers, the cynics and the cheapskates. Then there are those who insist on laughing at all the wrong moments, strangely humourless during the funnies, invariably finding graphic descriptions of torture rib-tickling. It's a mixed bag indeed. I thought after many years I had seen it all, that is until one evening when a family from Glasgow turned up. There is something peculiar about the mind set of certain Glaswegians, I have found. For example, some on meeting often ignore the traditional swopping of names or handshake in greeting preferring to state, I'm from Glesga' by the way.' These words are invariably proffered not as a fact but as a threat and perhaps it's a test of ones working class credentials that you can take that first volley on the chin.

And so, on arrival at the meeting point on that fateful evening I noticed with distaste two aged drunken men, tattooed and toothless lying sprawled across the pavement. They had between them a carryout of epic proportions; a load so prodigious that even Hannibal would have baulked at transporting it. Making themselves quite at home they lounged inelegantly against a nearby bollard where they spoke in harsh guttural tones. I wrongly assumed they were just two of Edinburgh's merry layabouts of which there are many. With our newfound companions, myself and John the supervisor, now waited pensively. It was still early and

bitterly cold, the wind sweeping up from the closes only adding to the forlorn spectacle. Moments later I noticed a large
crowd making their way up the street and I squinted to dis-
cern their features from afar. They were a motley bunch consisting of around six or so gentlemen, possibly mid-twenties,
four young ladies approximately of similar age all led by a
matriarchal figure. The overriding impression I got a first
glance did not fill me with joy, as I heard snatches of bickering
amongst the clink of bottles. As they neared it was apparent,
they had been at one with Bacchus whose spell had cast a
surly demeanour upon them. But worse was to come, as on
espying the group the two gentlemen who had up till then
remained horizontally on the kerb, flickered into life and
shouted a greeting towards the new arrivals. Did they know
each other I wondered? The plot thickened. I was enlightened
mere seconds later after finding out they were 'the grandfa-
thers.' I concede they were not your Werther's sucking cosy
cardigan and slippers type grandad, but rather the Buckfast
stained lips and a bunch of fives variety, however grandfa-
thers they were. My heart sank as the group approached and
after a brief unintelligible conversation, I was assured that despite their 'high spirits' they were looking forward to the tour.
So, like a man awaiting execution I now stood as the nearby
Tron clock interminably ticked towards the appointed hour.
A tortoise with an anvil attached to its testicles could not have
crawled more slowly than those last few minutes but in due
course I was given the nod.

Today, three years later I still can't adequately convey the
sheer horror of the situation and even today when thinking of
it my stomach tightens. Perhaps it was the constant cat calling
throughout my storytelling, the hassling of innocent passers-
by or the looks of innate violence? Perhaps it was one fellow's

use of a discarded traffic cone, who kept a running commentary throughout, that set me on edge? Maybe it was bellowing through said cone into my face, that was the clincher? It was all these things and more. 'O don't mind him,' said mother, reading my obvious discomfort, 'he's just playing up.' I was not re-assured, and to this day I still don't know why I didn't just run. Worse of all though was the fact there were around seven other participants on the tour, mere innocents, including a family from Spain who remained cowed and fearful throughout. The song 'Spanish Eyes,' was perhaps written to convey the emotions found within those dark orbs that evening, yet it failed to convey the anguish I witnessed, as he glanced at me beseechingly. I was powerless to help. What could I do? If those Glaswegians had worked for the tourist board it would have been the death nell for the Scottish economy, of that, I'm sure. To go into any more detail would dimply invoke bad memories, and though one is told not to suppress traumatic events or associated feelings I feel in this case it is best left alone. Suffice to say that at the conclusion, the tour being a little shorter than usual, a few brief handshakes were exchanged before the location of the nearest supermarket secured. Watching from the darkened entrance to Greyfriars Kirk, I observed the stumbling crowd as they lurched towards Sainsburys having drained the remains of their carry out on route. They of course paid me nothing though I was paid in kindness for not being mugged. Once out of ear shot, I spent the next five minutes apologising to the rest of the party whose faces had the look of someone, who after a particularly arduous bout of constipation, had found relief. And that dear reader was my worst ghost tour ever.

Conclusion

There are not many places like Edinburgh, where one can immerse oneself in history so readily and so provides the perfect setting for those who feel drawn to an age when stories were told by candlelight and the night brought unexplained terrors. The creak of the floorboard, the scuttle of mouse and the billowing 'haar' all played their part, though the mysterious world that our ancestors lived in is now long gone. Today on the High Street one can easily slip into the past by traversing many of the closes off the mile, however the dark and dingy tenements are a thing of the past. Like their ghosts, the buildings outwardly appearances promise much, but sometimes cannot deliver. The old stories, have little to back them up though perhaps most were just old wife's tales to begin with. There is no written evidence of the exploits of the spirit of John Chielsey, pushing folk in Advocates Close, or actual eye-witness accounts of the phantom coach of Major Weir on West Bow, yet they still exist, frozen in time and curios from a different age. Interesting as many of these old tales are, and who doesn't enjoy a good story, I am personally drawn to more 'modern' accounts where there is always the chance of speaking to the protagonists first hand. Of course, that does not necessarily mean people will be willing to talk. Reticence is still common, and just as the protagonists of old worried over their reputations, the modern witness is also fearful of public humiliation, but now through social media. It has been stated that one out of three people in Britain believe in ghosts. It would be great to think so, but I am doubtful of those figures and so the question remains, does one have to believe in the afterlife to enjoy a good ghost story? Possibly not, but it might be helpful. For those who don't believe in the supernatural it is unlikely that you would have picked up this book, but for those who do or at least enjoy a little night-time reading, I hope you have enjoyed the tour. One last word of advice, if you are considering a career as a tour guide, you may wish to consider some of the points raised herein.

Some further reading

- New Town Nightmares: John S. Tantalon
- Elliot O' Donell: Scottish Ghosts/Dangerous Ghosts
- Edinburgh Evening News: Liam Rudden
- Edinburgh City of the Dead: Jan Andrew Henderson
- Haunted Edinburgh: Alan Murdie
- The Perambulator Around Edinburgh: William Bone
- Traditions of Edinburgh: Robert Chambers
- Satan's Invisible World Revealed: George Sinclair
- Perambulator in Edinburgh: James Bone 1911
- Total Darkness: Mark Edward Wilson
- Aberdeen's Haunted Heritage: Graeme Milne
- The Haunted North volumes 1 & 2: Graeme Milne.
- Edinburgh After Dark: Ron Halliday
- Poltergeist over Scotland: Geoff Holder

Index